SUMMER OF '64
A SEASON IN ENGLISH CRICKET

SUMMER OF '64
A SEASON IN ENGLISH CRICKET

ANDREW HIGNELL

TEMPUS

First published 2005

Tempus Publishing Limited
The Mill, Brimscombe Port,
Stroud, Gloucestershire, GL5 2QG
www.tempus-publishing.com

British Library Cataloguing in Publication Data.
A catalogue record for this book is available from the British Library.

ISBN 0 7524 3404 7

Typesetting and origination by Tempus Publishing Limited
Printed and bound in Great Britain

Contents

Foreword: '1964 and all that'
Memories of a glorious summer long past

by Peter Walker
(Glamorgan & England 1956-1972)

When Andrew Hignell asked me to contribute a few thoughts on the summer of '64 I had a momentary panic attack! At my age, memory is either sharpened, warped or blurred. Like most ex-professional cricketers, I fall securely into the latter category when attempting to recall individual seasons or memorable performances. Inevitably therefore I turned to Mike Fatkin, the indefatigable and highly efficient Glamorgan Cricket Chief Executive, a man with an elephantine memory. Mike was quick to point out that 1964 was the year he was born and at Swansea, on that very day, 23 May, Glamorgan's highest aggregate run scorer Alan Jones had taken 60 off an Essex attack that included the legendary Jim Laker in the twilight of his playing days and Robin Hobbs who, at a similar stage in his career, later moved due west to captain Glamorgan.

Confirmation of the details of the match in the county's yearbook drew my attention to the fact that during the match P.M. Walker, batting at number six, scored 35 and 2 not out, took 1 wicket for 11 runs in 8 overs opening the bowling with Ossie Wheatley and disappointingly held but a single catch in the two Essex innings. Scorecards do provide a marvellous memory prompt. The Glamorgan batting line-up for that match, and for much of the '64 season, is a list of well-remembered names: Alan Jones, Bernard Hedges, Tony Lewis, Alan Rees, Jim Pressdee, Peter Walker, Euros Lewis, Gwyn Hughes, David Evans, Don Shepherd (nine wickets in the match, won by Glamorgan by six wickets) and Ossie Wheatley, our captain.

Three days prior to the Essex match the county had fought out a draw against the Australians at Cardiff Arms Park, a game that included an innings of 109 by Norman O'Neill that ranks as one of the finest I've ever seen. As the then seventeenth and youngest first-class county (that status achieved in 1921), Glamorgan benefited from the fact that the Whitsun and August Bank Holiday fixture lists were set in concrete with long-standing local derbies between the other sixteen counties often dating back to the nineteenth century! These were sacrosanct and not to be tampered with. Therefore, two very financially lucrative games against the touring side each season fell into grateful laps on the Welsh side of the Bristol Channel.

The second meeting in early August 1964 against Australia in what was locally described as 'the Sixth Test – Wales versus Australia' ended in a famous home win. Reviewing the season in the 1965 Yearbook, Wilfred Wooller described it as, 'the greatest single victory in the history of the club'. It gave the club a 'full house' of victories against all the major touring sides, but the one against Australia held a special place. It had dawned overcast but dry on 1 August 1964, the pitch its normal St Helen's colour, light brown with a potential to dust. Captain Ossie Wheatley's decision to bat recognised that

Peter Walker.

it would become 'a typical Swansea turner' and the side batting last would be sorely pressed to save the game. But at 50 for 3, it needed a partnership of length and productivity. Your author, with 41, and Alan Rees, the former Wales outside half, with 48 pushed the total up to 150 before the next Glamorgan wicket fell, but then a collapse left the county totalling a modest 197. Significantly for the outcome of the match, Australian off-spinner Tom Veivers had taken 5/85; significant as Glamorgan's main strike bowler was Don Shepherd, arguably the finest off-spinner of his day.

The first innings of Australia, however, was a triumph for left-arm spinner Jim Pressdee. Alongside his 6/58 in 15.2 overs, Shepherd contributed 4/22 from 17 typically run-strangling pinpoint accurate overs. Australia: 101 all out. Glamorgan's second innings of 172 was built from a stylish 36 by Tony Lewis batting at number three and yet another pugnacious 47 from Rees. Needing 269 to win a match in which no side had topped 200 proved too much for the tourists and with Shepherd (5/71) in no less than 52 overs and Pressdee 4/65 in 28.1, in front of 10,000 fired-up spectators Glamorgan swept to a 36-run historic victory. For the Aussies, a second-innings haul of 3/65 plus innings of 51 and 54 from Tom Veivers would have certainly won him the Man of the Match award in modern times.

History was to repeat itself in 1968 with Glamorgan again winning in Swansea. As Barry Jarman, then captain of Australia and wicketkeeper in 1964, said to the crowd of some 7,000 who had gathered in front of the pavilion at the end of the game to salute both teams for a splendid game of cricket, 'So, we've been beaten by Glamorgan – what's new?'

Peter Walker – the young batsman at
Cardiff Arms Park in 1956.

If the first ever win over Australia proved to be the high point of the 1964 season,
Glamorgan ended up a disappointing eleventh in the Championship table after finishing second the year before. But there were some memorable other moments con-
cerning English cricket that summer. Although Australia won the Test series, Yorkshire
fast bowler Fred Trueman became the first man in history to take 300 Test wickets
when he had Neil Hawke caught by Colin Cowdrey in the Oval Test. *Wisden*'s select-
ed 'Five Cricketers of the Year' included three Australians: Bobby Simpson, Peter Burge
and Graham McKenzie, plus England's Geoffrey Boycott (Yorkshire), and Jack Flavell
(Worcestershire). Another milestone was the post-war period's most elegant batsman
Tom Graveney reaching a century of centuries playing for Worcestershire, the county
he had gravitated to from Gloucestershire. Unsurprisingly they won the County
Championship for the first time in their history. A massive 41 points separated them
from second-placed Warwickshire and was built around a high-class opening bowling
pair of Flavell and Len Coldwell, supported by a quality group of close catchers including Ron Headley and Dick Richardson.

If there is a fundamental difference between the professional game of forty years ago
compared to today, it's in the way in which, away from the bat, fielding and throwing
has vastly improved but this improvement has been matched by an equally dramatic
decline in close-catching skills. Why? Simply because uncovered pitches encouraged
attacking bowling and aggressive field placings at the expense of run-saving. The position in today's game, played on basically flat, bland, fully covered surfaces, has shifted
the onus onto run prevention rather than wicket-taking.

Peter Walker in bowling mode.

Legendary cricketers who passed on in 1964 to be recorded by 'the Great Scorer in the Sky' included George Brown, the Hampshire and England all-rounder, aged seventy-seven. In a career either side of the First World War he scored 25,649 runs, took 629 wickets and as a part-time wicketkeeper, held 458 catches and made 50 stumpings! Another notable departee mentioned in *Wisden*'s despatches was 'Peter', a black cat who spent twelve of his fourteen years prowling the outfield at Lord's. *Wisden* solemnly noted he had enjoyed the last of his nine lives in the late summer of '64!

Reading such gems, one's memory is jolted awake. Those days of long, long ago become once again fresh and relevant. Abiding memories of the crowd singing Glamorgan and Wales to victory against the Australians at St Helens, and of Peter the cat turning his back on a particularly dull period of play and disappearing into the Long Room with nary a backward glance once again become like yesterday. Peter the cat was reckoned to be a shrewd judge at a time when cricket, full of idiosyncrasies and foibles, was unquestionably England's national summer game.

Peter Walker
Christmas 2004

Preface and
Acknowledgements

1964 was the year when The Beatles made their first visit to the United States, only a few months after the American President John Fitzgerald Kennedy had been assassinated during a motorcade through the Texan city of Dallas. 1964 was also the year when the *Sun* newspaper was first published in the UK, and *Top of the Pops* was first broadcast on British television. It was the year when Harold Wilson was elected British Prime Minister, when Peter Sellers and Britt Ekland were married in London, and the year when the film *Mary Poppins* won a series of Oscars. On a wider stage, it was also the year when Nelson Mandela was sentenced to life in prison for opposing apartheid. On the sporting front, it was the year when the Olympics were staged in Tokyo, the capital city of the newly emerging nation of Japan, while on the football fields of the UK, West Ham United dramatically defeated Preston North End 3-2 in the final of the FA Cup in front of a packed house at Wembley Stadium.

Events on the cricket fields of England, and Wales, were no less dramatic, and this book turns the clock back to those sunny summer days over forty years ago when one-day cricket was in its infancy. It was the summer when Bobby Simpson's Australians visited these shores, and before they had even arrived they were being written off as one of the weakest Australian sides to contest an Ashes series. But they proceeded to refute these assertions and returned home with the Ashes in their safekeeping. Yet despite enjoying a successful time in the Test series, they also lost their county matches to both Warwickshire and Glamorgan, with the latter match at Swansea, being almost akin to an extra Test match against the might of Wales! All of these events are recalled, alongside the triumph of Worcestershire in becoming the Champion County for 1964. The feats of their bowlers and batsmen, including Tom Graveney who notched up his 100th century during the course of the summer, are all recounted in detail, as well as the feats of Sussex in winning the Gillette Cup under the leadership of England's captain 'Lord Ted' Dexter.

This book also looks at other individuals, notably Fred Trueman, who hit cricket's headlines in 1964, as he became the first man in cricket history to take 300 Test wickets. His feats, in addition to a number of rising stars, are lavishly recalled, as are the venues at which these county games were staged over forty years ago. Many of these grounds no longer appear on the cricket calendar, but their place in the chronicle of county cricket of 1964 are duly recorded in this lavishly illustrated book.

My thanks to former England and Glamorgan cricketer Peter Walker for writing the foreword, while I am grateful for the assistance of the following who have helped provide reminiscences or photographs for this book – Autographica, David Baggett,

Robert Brooke, Central Press Agency, Stephen Chalke, Roger Davis, Tom Graveney, the late Les Hatton, George Heringshaw, Vic Isaacs, Peter James, Alan Jones, Ray Julian, Keystone Press Agency, Dennis Lambert, Jerry Lodge, Rev. Malcolm Lorimer, Kevin Lyons, Douglas Miller, Mark Newton, the late Frank Peach, Don Shepherd, Bill Smith, Sport and General Press Agency, *Western Mail and Echo*, Ossie Wheatley, the late Wilf Wooller and Peter Wynne-Thomas. My thanks also to the librarians and archivists at Surrey CCC, Worcestershire CCC, Nottinghamshire CCC and Gloucestershire CCC.

Every attempt has been made to trace ownership and copyright for the photographs used in this book. Apologies to anyone who has inadvertently been omitted.

Andrew Hignell
St Fagans, Cardiff
February 2005

Tom Graveney
A Century of Hundreds

The date 5 August 1964 was a red-letter day for Tom Graveney, as he became the fifteenth batsman in cricket history to score 100 hundreds, with a typically sublime 132 in Worcestershire's first innings of their Championship contest against Northamptonshire at New Road.

As Tom later recalled, 'the day was warm and on a turning wicket, Northamptonshire bowled their two left-handers, David Steele and Malcolm Scott, for most of the time. My innings was long, more a test of patience, and runs did not come too quickly. I remember creeping onto 99, and I had to face David Larter, their giant fast bowler, for a full over. I have played with and against Larter on many occasions and I knew that he could be dangerous. But on that day he had not bowled well, and it is fair to say he was all over the place. At least he was until that over to me – the first 5 balls of the over were very fast and very accurate, and it was all I could do to keep them away from my wicket. The sixth was a head-high bouncer – head-high to my six feet – which I managed to hook down in front of short leg and the ball bounced over him towards fine leg for the one run that I wanted. There was plenty of cheering and Larter led the bunch of players who congratulated me. It was a great feeling because I had wondered, at one stage, whether I was ever going to hit a century again.'

Many glowing tributes were paid to Graveney following his feat, with Neville Cardus writing in the 1965 *Wisden* that Graveney 'has no equal as a complete and stylish strokeplayer. Ted Dexter can outshine him in rhetoric, so to say; Roy Marshall in virtuosity of execution, but neither Dexter nor Marshall is Graveney's superior in point of effortless balance. When he is in form, Graveney makes batsmanship look the easiest and most natural thing in the world. An innings of Graveney remains in the memory. Simply by closing our eyes we can still see, in deep winter as we browse by the fire in twilight, a stroke by Graveney; we can see and delight in the free uplift of his bat, the straight lissom poise and the rhythm of his swinging drives.'

Tom's first-class career had begun with Gloucestershire after the Second World War. After his National Service ended in 1947, Tom initially had the opportunity to train as an accountant, but instead he opted for a career in sport, and after turning down an offer to become a professional golfer, he decided to join his elder brother Ken on the Gloucestershire staff. Despite making 0 on his county debut in 1948, Tom was soon delighting the crowds at Bristol, and other county grounds, with his elegant strokeplay. In 1951 he made his Test debut for England, and the following year he became one of *Wisden*'s Five Cricketers of the Year. He took over the Gloucestershire captaincy in 1959, but some of the county's officials felt that the captaincy was inhibiting

Above: Tom Graveney returns to the Worcester pavilion after scoring the 100th century of his career.

Left: Tom Graveney.

his strokeplay. A few undercurrents existed at what was a sorry time for the West Country side and Graveney left the Bristol club in 1960.

The internal wranglings left their mark on a man who a few seasons before had been a fairly uncomplicated and easy-going individual. Observers believe that Tom became a much more ruthless and less frivolous batsman in the subsequent years, as Gloucestershire's loss became Worcestershire's gain. After appearing for Worcestershire against the Australian tourists and Cambridge University in 1961, Tom completed his qualification period and in May 1962 he made his Championship debut for his new club against Sussex at Hove.

Tom enjoyed a vintage summer in 1964 as Worcestershire became County Champions, and as Trevor Bailey commented 'it is doubtful if one single batsman has ever exerted as much influence on the outcome as Tom did for Worcester in 1964. He carried the batting and scored over 2,000 runs. However, he also steered his side to reasonable totals when the pressure was on, and the pitch was poor. Without him, his county would never have triumphed.'

Tom Graveney – His Route to 100 Hundreds

1948	114	Gloucestershire *v.* Combined Services	at Gloucester
1949	159	Gloucestershire *v.* Somerset	at Bristol
	139	Gloucestershire *v.* Nottinghamshire	at Trent Bridge
	132	Gloucestershire *v.* Surrey	at The Oval
	108	Gloucestershire *v.* Oxford University	at The Parks
1950	201	Gloucestershire *v.* Sussex	at Worthing
	197	Gloucestershire *v.* Nottinghamshire	at Bristol
	115	Gloucestershire *v.* Glamorgan	at Gloucester
1951	201	Gloucestershire *v.* Oxford University	at The Parks
	146	Gloucestershire *v.* Surrey	at The Oval
	128	Gloucestershire *v.* Warwickshire	at Bristol
	113	Gloucestershire *v.* Nottinghamshire	at Trent Bridge
	107	Gloucestershire *v.* Leicestershire	at Bristol
	103	Gloucestershire *v.* Northamptonshire	at Bristol
	105★	Gloucestershire *v.* Northamptonshire	at Bristol
	104	Gloucestershire *v.* Oxford University	at Bristol
1951/52	175	England *v.* India	at Bombay
	123	MCC *v.* Pakistan	at Karachi
	109★	MCC *v.* Pakistan	at Lahore
	102★	MCC *v.* Ceylon	at Colombo
	101	MCC *v.* Combined Universities	at Bombay
	101	MCC *v.* Services	at Dehra Dun

Tom Graveney, with many other prominent cricketers in the Rest of England side that played Surrey at the Scarborough Festival in September 1957: F.H. Tyson, P.E. Richardson, D.C.S. Compton, D.W. Richardson, T.W. Graveney, T.E. Bailey (captain), F.S. Trueman, T.G. Evans, J.H. Wardle, R.E. Marshall and G.E. Tribe.

1952	171	Gloucestershire *v.* Sussex	at Bristol
	166★	Gloucestershire *v.* Leicestershire	at Leicester
	158	MCC *v.* India	at Lord's
	113★	Gloucestershire *v.* Somerset	at Bristol
	105	Gloucestershire *v.* Cambridge University	at Bristol
	104	Gloucestershire *v.* Worcestershire	at Worcester
1953	211	Gloucestershire *v.* Kent	at Gillingham
	126★	Gloucestershire *v.* Leicestershire	at Bristol
	124	Gloucestershire *v.* Oxford University	at Oxford
	110★	Gloucestershire *v.* Somerset	at Bristol
1953/54	231	MCC *v.* British Guiana	at Georgetown
1954	222	Gloucestershire *v.* Derbyshire	at Chesterfield
	177★	Gloucestershire *v.* Glamorgan	at Gloucester
	125★	Gloucestershire *v.* Northamptonshire	at Northampton
	111★	Gloucestershire *v.* Essex	at Gloucester
	107	Gloucestershire *v.* Somerset	at Taunton
1954/55	134	MCC *v.* Tasmania	at Launceston
	111	England *v.* Australia	at Sydney
	102	MCC *v.* Wellington	at Wellington
	101	MCC *v.* Canterbury	at Christchurch

Tom Graveney with his wife Jackie, son Timothy and daughter Rebecca, after he had received the OBE from the Queen at Buckingham Palace in 1968.

1955	159	T.N. Pearce's XI *v.* South Africans	at Scarborough
	128	Gloucestershire *v.* Worcestershire	at Worcester
	104	Gloucestershire *v.* Somerset	at Taunton
	101	Gloucestershire *v.* Northamptonshire	at Kettering
	101	MCC *v.* Yorkshire	at Scarborough
1955/56	154	E.W. Swanton's XI *v.* Barbados	at Bridgetown
	117	E.W. Swanton's XI *v.* Trinidad	at Port-of-Spain
1956	200	Gloucestershire *v.* Glamorgan	at Newport
	190	Gloucestershire *v.* Leicestershire	at Bristol
	156	Gloucestershire *v.* Middlesex	at Gloucester
	152	Gloucestershire *v.* Middlesex	at Lord's
	133	Gloucestershire *v.* Somerset	at Bristol
	124	Players *v.* Gentlemen	at Scarborough
	112	MCC *v.* Yorkshire	at Lord's
	101	T.N. Pearce's XI *v.* Australians	at Scarborough
	100	Gloucestershire *v.* Essex	at Romford
1956/57	153	C.G. Howard's XI *v.* Cricket Club of India	at Bombay
	120	C.G. Howard's XI *v.* Cricket Club of India	at Bombay
1957	258	England *v.* West Indies	at Trent Bridge
	164	England *v.* West Indies	at The Oval

	134	Gloucestershire *v.* Somerset	at Bristol
	122	Gloucestershire *v.* Warwickshire	at Bristol
	111★	Gloucestershire *v.* Worcestershire	at Bristol
	106	Gloucestershire *v.* Warwickshire	at Edgbaston
	101★	Gloucestershire *v.* Warwickshire	at Edgbaston
	101★	Gloucestershire *v.* Middlesex	at Lord's
1958	156	Gloucestershire *v.* Essex	at Bristol
	114	Gloucestershire *v.* Northamptonshire	at Gloucester
1958/59	177★	MCC *v.* Western Australia	at Perth
	108	MCC *v.* Northern and Central Districts	at Hamilton
1959	155★	Gloucestershire *v.* Nottinghamshire	at Trent Bridge
1959/60	102★	Commonwealth XI *v.* Invitation XI	at Johannesburg
	100★	Commonwealth XI *v.* Combined XI	at Pretoria
1960	142★	Gloucestershire *v.* Middlesex	at Cheltenham
	135	Gloucestershire *v.* Derbyshire	at Chesterfield
1960/61	105	Commonwealth XI *v.* Combined XI	at Johannesburg
1961	152★	Worcestershire *v.* Cambridge University	at Cambridge
	124	Col. Steven's XI *v.* Cambridge University	at Eastbourne
1961/62	116★	International XI *v.* New Zealand President's XI	at Auckland
	112★	International XI *v.* Rhodesian XI	at Nkana
1962	164★	Worcestershire *v.* Somerset	at Worcester
	153	England *v.* Pakistan	at Lord's
	147★	Worcestershire *v.* Middlesex	at Worcester
	119	Worcestershire *v.* Middlesex	at Lord's
	117	Worcestershire *v.* Pakistan	at Worcester
	115	Worcestershire *v.* Northamptonshire	at Kidderminster
	114	England *v.* Pakistan	at Trent Bridge
	110	MCC *v.* Pakistan	at Lord's
	106	Worcestershire *v.* Hampshire	at Worcester
1962/63	185	MCC *v.* Victoria	at Melbourne
	122★	MCC *v.* South Australia	at Adelaide
1963	100	Worcestershire *v.* Derbyshire	at Worcester
	164	International XI *v.* Pakistan	at Lahore
	107★	International XI *v.* Pakistan	at Lahore
1963/64	108★	Cavaliers *v.* Jamaica	at Kingston

1964	122★	Worcestershire *v.* Yorkshire	at Scarborough
	109	Worcestershire *v.* Leicestershire	at Worcester
	132	Worcestershire *v.* Northamptonshire	at Worcester

Graveney also scored 106 *v.* Essex at Leyton and 164 *v.* Nottinghamshire at Worcester in 1964 after reaching the milestone of 100 first-class hundreds.

Wonderful Worcestershire

The graceful batting of Tom Graveney was one of the decisive elements behind Worcestershire's Championship success. But, as Graveney himself wrote in his memoirs, 'many factors contribute to the production of a side that wins the County Championship – we were a very well balanced side and nearly every time we had to call on a reserve, particularly in bowling, it proved to be successful. Without a doubt we were wonderfully led by Don Kenyon. Right from the word go, Don proved what I had always thought him to be – a steady, solid and unworried character – and even in the most tense of situations, Don remained Don. He was calm and unruffled in that bad spell when we lost three matches out of four. Don maintained that we were not to be put off by defeat, providing we were beaten going for victory. He reckoned that more good and more points would result if we adopted this attitude. Events proved him completely right.'

Much of the club's success in 1964 was down to the inspired leadership of Don Kenyon, but like all success in sport, the seeds had been sown over the previous seasons. 1964 therefore saw Kenyon reap the rewards for his efforts in the preceding years, having taken over the captaincy in 1959 following Peter Richardson's decision to move to Kent. Kenyon proved himself to be a fine captain, carrying out his duties with great zest and tactical acumen, and like all of the truly great leaders in county cricket, he was always prepared to lead by example or deed. With a sharp eye, and quick reflexes, Kenyon always showed a forthright approach when batting. He loved to dominate opposing attacks with a bat that seemed to the tiring bowlers to be one of the broadest in the country. His appetite for run-scoring was almost insatiable, and by the time Kenyon retired from the county game in 1967, he had scored more runs and hit more centuries for the county than any other player in Worcestershire's history. While his ruddy countenance looked as though it belonged to a Malvern farmer, there was certainly nothing rustic in his batting style – in fact quite the reverse, as Kenyon possessed a truly magnificent repertoire of classical strokes. His cultured batting matched the serene and dignified surroundings of the New Road ground, and his glorious shots thrilled and enraptured several generations of schoolboys.

The side that Kenyon took over had met with little success during the 1950s, and since 1952 the New Road club had finished no higher than ninth in the Championship table. His first couple of seasons had seen few signs of improvement, but a turning point came in 1961 when his team recorded no less than sixteen victories and rose up to fourth place in the table. Four bowlers – Jack Flavell, Len Coldwell, Norman Gifford and Martin Horton – all took over 100 wickets, while Horton also achieved the Double with 1,808 runs and 101 wickets in all first-class games.

WORCESTER CATHEDRAL FROM THE CRICKET GROUND

Above: The New Road
ground – a most tranquil
setting.

Right: Don Kenyon.

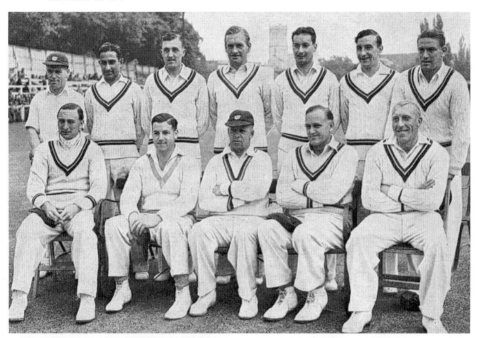

Clockwise from top:

Don Kenyon in the Worcestershire side of 1949. From left to right, standing: H. Yarnold,
L. Outschoorn, E. Cooper, R. Howorth, D. Kenyon, F. Cooper, R.O. Jenkins. Sitting: R.E. Bird,
A.F.T. White, R.E.S. Wyatt, R.T.D. Perks, P.F. Jackson.

Roy Booth.

Another four for Ron Headley.

All of the bowlers were ably supported by the Worcestershire fielders, while the club's wicketkeeper, Roy Booth, also emerged as a craftsman of the highest quality. Whereas some county 'keepers opted for a flamboyant style, Booth developed a more unobtrusive, but equally effective approach, and his immaculate glovework was a source of great confidence for his bowlers. Booth had moved from Yorkshire in 1956, and after a short trial, he cemented a regular place in the side. He was no slouch with the bat either, and for three successive seasons, 1959 to 1961, he came close to the rare feat of the wicketkeeping 'Double' of 1,000 runs and 100 dismissals.

On the batting front, 1961 saw Ron Headley, the son of West Indian legend George Headley, prove himself to be a match-winning batsman. With plenty of Caribbean flair, the gifted strokemaker amassed over 2,000 runs, and showed himself to be a thrilling, and at times ferocious, straight driver of the ball. Many county bowlers felt the force of Headley's batting, as on many occasions in 1961 he immediately took the attack to the bowlers and sought to dominate them right from the outset.

The following year, 1962, saw Tom Graveney enjoy a productive first season in Worcestershire colours. The former Gloucestershire batsman scored 2,269 runs, as Worcestershire consolidated on their improved form and came agonisingly close to winning the title. Celebrations had begun and the champagne corks were popping after a victory over Nottinghamshire But the celebrations proved to be premature, as Yorkshire pipped Worcestershire for the title. While the senior Worcestershire side came within 5 points of securing the title, the county's Second XI won the Second XI Championship in 1962, and confirmed that there were some talented young cricketers waiting in the wings at New Road. The club's youngsters repeated the trick in 1963, and their continued success somewhat atoned for the First XI's slip down to fifteenth position in the County Championship. The feeling though was that this had been a blip, and these views were confirmed in 1964 as Kenyon's men put the record straight and brought the Championship pennant to New Road for the first time in the club's history.

In all, Worcestershire won eighteen of their twenty-eight Championship matches in 1964, and proved themselves to be worthy champions after having a dogfight at the top of the table with Warwickshire throughout the second half of the season. In fact, it was not until 7 August that Worcestershire got their noses in front, but once there, they remained at the top of the table, winning seven out of their last eight matches, while Warwickshire could only register three wins in their final seven games. By the time the season ended, the New Road club had extended their lead to a more emphatic 41 points, and few quibbled that the best team had become County Champions.

The summer had begun quite modestly, as Worcestershire lost narrowly to Glamorgan at Newport in the first round of the Gillette Cup, followed by a draw against Australia, but then in the space of the next fourteen days, they launched their Championship season with four consecutive victories. They began by beating Lancashire at Old Trafford by 56 runs on a wicket where the spinners prospered throughout. After Worcestershire had slipped to 69 for 4, Graveney and Duncan Fearnley both hit seventies to see their side to a more respectable total. As it turned out, 226 proved to be a match-winning total, as Lancashire were then dismissed for 96, before Jack Flavell took 4/37 on the final day as Lancashire failed in their quest for 240. Then Middlesex were defeated at Lord's by five wickets as the home side dramatically collapsed in their second innings after securing a first-innings lead of 18. They lost 3 early wickets on the second evening, before losing a further 7 for just 23 on the final morning, with Len Coldwell taking 7/25 as Middlesex were dismissed for a meagre 54. Coldwell continued his good form as Glamorgan's visit to New Road ended in an innings defeat inside two days. Coldwell finished with ten wickets in the match, while Kenyon, Horton and Headley all scored half-centuries. The fourth victory came as Leicestershire were beaten at Grace Road by 44 runs, after a real gamble by Kenyon had paid off, and had proved the wisdom of the Worcestershire captain. As Graveney later wrote, 'no team that wins the Championship can do so without taking chances. We had to take justifiable risks to stay in the chase, and one gamble was at Leicester – a match hit by rain – when we gave ourselves ninety minutes to bowl Leicestershire out. We had offered Leicestershire a challenge too, setting them 120 in the time, but the wicket, a real Grace Road turner, was in our favour. I still thought it would be difficult to bowl them out in time, but we succeeded, thanks mainly to Norman Gifford (who took 7/31 in the home team's second innings).'

But the winning run came to a soggy halt when they returned to Worcester for the visit of Yorkshire. Kenyon hit a fine 113, while Graveney struck a sparkling 68, but the weather proved to be the only winner as the game ended in a draw. However, Worcestershire soon returned to winning ways as their visit to Dartford produced an emphatic victory over Kent by 230 runs. Headley starred with the bat, recording an

Len Coldwall.

Norman Gifford leading out the
Worcestershire side in the early 1970s,
followed by Brian Brain and Basil d'Oliveira.

unbeaten 117 inside three hours, before catching the last four Kent batsmen at short
leg as the home team failed by some margin in their quest of 346 on the final day.
With Worcestershire riding high in the table, 8,000 people shoehorned themselves into
the New Road ground for the visit of Sussex. The partisan locals were eager to wit-
ness their heroes prove themselves against a county side led by England captain Ted
Dexter, and the home supporters were not disappointed as Horton made a steady 116
before Richardson blasted a quick-fire 103. There was further good news the next
morning as Flavell was included in the England party for the First Test, and he duly
celebrated by dismissing 'Lord Ted' on the second morning, but after only 8 overs had
been bowled, storms rolled down from the Malvern Hills and washed out the rest of
the match.

Morale was high in the Worcester camp, and this spirit helped them to maintain
their winning form at Chesterfield, but only just, as the match with Derbyshire proved
to be a real cliffhanger. The inclement weather interfered with play again on the first
two days, so in an attempt to make up for lost time, Kenyon declared before the start
of the final day with his side 113 runs in arrears. After a brief second-innings flurry,
Derbyshire set Worcestershire a target of 174 in even time. It looked rather like a generous offer as Graveney raced to 60, but after his dismissal, wickets fell at regular intervals against the steady Derby attack. The rain clouds were also gathering as the final
pair, Norman Gifford and Bob Carter, came together with 8 runs still needed from a
handful of overs. Even though rain started to fall, the two tail-enders held their nerve,
with Carter hitting the winning runs off the penultimate delivery.

Left: Jack Flavell.

Opposite page, left: Doug Slade.

Opposite page, right: Jim Standen.

The rain followed the joyous Worcester team to the Arms Park in Cardiff, and although the first day's play was washed out, the weather gods could not stop another comprehensive victory over Glamorgan. Jim Standen came up trumps in the first innings, claiming seven wickets, and moving the ball deceptively off the seam on the worn surface, before some bold strokeplay by Headley, Kenyon and Horton against the Welsh bowlers saw the visitors to a nine-wicket win. This victory at Cardiff was the first major contribution in 1964 from Jim Standen – the likeable and popular medium-pacer who mixed county cricket in the summer with keeping goal for West Ham United during the winter. As befitted a professional footballer, Standen was a superbly fit and agile sportsman, whose talents as a cricketer were more than just as a bowler. In the outfield, Standen caught practically everything within his reach, and on occasions he clung onto balls that he should not have. He was a valuable lower-order batsman, who could score runs quickly and was not overawed by opposing bowlers. He arrived at New Road in the early summer with an FA Cup winners' medal in his pocket, and by the time the summer was over, and he was back with The Hammers at Upton Park, Jim had played a significant role in Worcestershire becoming County Champions.

Worcestershire's target at Cardiff had been a rather modest 109 – in the following game at The Oval, they were set a much stiffer one of 237 in a fraction over two-and-a-half hours, and all on a wearing wicket. The Surrey spinners induced several edges, but the fielders could not hold onto the chances, and Graveney was twice reprieved as he set his side on the way with 64. Further wickets quickly fell, and it was left to Doug Slade to mount a rearguard action and preserve Worcester's unbeaten tag.

By mid-June Worcestershire and Warwickshire were neck and neck at the top of the table, and with the two sides meeting each other at New Road, a crowd of 13,000 attended the first day's play in the local derby. At the time, it was the best for a Championship match at Worcester and it was the most seen inside the ground since the visit of the 1948 Australians. But the contest proved to be much less of a spectacle than many had anticipated as neither side gave the other an inch. After Worcestershire, who had batted first, had secured a one-run lead on first innings, a cultured 92 from Kenyon anchored their reply. Richardson also made a disciplined 91, as the home team extended their lead on the final day beyond 200. But the defensive fields employed by Warwickshire, coupled with their accurate bowling, meant that the Worcestershire batsmen were unable to score quickly enough to allow Kenyon to declare. His bowlers were never going to have enough time to bowl Warwickshire out again, so the game meandered to a draw, with the reputations of both teams still intact.

The next three days offered some light relief away from the cut and thrust of the Championship race as Worcestershire entertained Cambridge University on the county's inaugural visit to Halesowen. The students were never at ease against the county attack, and after acting captain Martin Horton had become the first batsman to a thousand, Worcestershire strolled to a ten-wicket win. The winning run continued in the next game against Somerset on the Imperial Ground in south Bristol. The game proved to be a good one for Brian Brain, who returned match figures of 10/166, but well as the young seamer bowled, his team's winning margin of 122 runs was helped greatly by the absence of Somerset's two strike bowlers in the visitors' second innings. Ken Palmer was unable to bowl because of a back strain, and then

Don Kenyon.

Fred Rumsey pulled up with a leg injury after 8 overs. Without their best two bowlers, Worcestershire's batsmen had the freedom to score quickly, and unlike the match with Warwickshire, there was ample time for Brain and Standen to bowl their side to victory.

After an innings victory over Oxford University, Kenyon's men maintained their fine form as Derbyshire visited New Road, although for a while on the final day, it looked as if the Peakites might end Worcester's winning sequence. The wicket assisted the seamers throughout, but the home batting fell away rather indifferently in their second innings, and a few of the Worcester pessimists had started to shake their heads as the visiting batsmen began their quest of 114 on the final afternoon. However, their doubts were allayed as Coldwell produced a superb spell of swing bowling. The Derbyshire batsmen found him almost unplayable, as they slumped to 35 for 7, before a counterattack by Edwin Smith and Peter Eyre briefly gave the Derby men a glimmer of hope. But Standen then replaced Carter and polished off the resistance, taking 3/3 in 2 overs as the visitors ended 43 runs short of their target.

Worcestershire then travelled to Edgbaston for the return match with Warwickshire, and with both counties still riding high in the table, all concerned knew that it was going to be an important encounter. The pitch proved to be one of rather variable bounce, and both Tom Cartwright and Rudi Webster exploited these vagaries as Worcestershire were dismissed for 119. But the home side then faired even worse as they limped to 72 all out in 42 overs as Standen took 6/45. It was a highly

Tom Graveney in majestic form.

commendable performance from the Worcester man because as well as demons in the wicket, Standen had to overcome a few doubts over his ability as a new-ball bowler. The seamer had a very light grip on the ball, and preferred not to open the bowling in case the ball slipped out from his fingers. But in the absence of the injured Coldwall, he rose to the occasion.

Another low total seemed on the cards as Worcestershire slumped to 27 for 2 in their second innings, but the complexion of the game was completely transformed as Graveney and Headley shared a fine partnership of 124 in two-and-a-half hours, and left the home team ruing the fact that Webster and David Brown had picked up niggles and could not bowl flat out. The watchfulness of the Worcester batsmen allowed them to build what proved to be a decisive lead, and Graveney was five short of a richly deserved hundred when his innings ended. The target of 306 in five hours proved to be a merely academic one as Gifford and Horton filleted the Warwickshire batting, as the home team were dismissed for 86 to hand Worcestershire a crucial victory.

The evening of 14 July was the first time during 1964 that Worcestershire had occupied top spot in the county table. But their joy at being in first place was short-lived, as their unbeaten run came to an abrupt end on their return to New Road for the match with Somerset, who ended up the deserved winners by 83 runs. None of the home batsmen found batting easy, yet when Somerset's men went to the crease, Merv Kitchen came within 2 runs of recording a maiden hundred, while in the second innings, Roy Virgin made a steadfast hundred that allowed Somerset to set

Worcestershire a target of 265 in three-and-a-quarter hours. The dry wicket proved to be an ideal surface for Brian Langford's canny off spin, and a Worcestershire defeat was on the cards as Langford dismissed Fearnley and Richardson with a pair of spiteful deliveries. He duly finished off the innings by taking the last 4 wickets at a cost of just 5 runs, as Worcestershire suffered their first Championship defeat of the summer.

Hopes of a quick return to winning ways were dashed in the following match at Dudley where rain prevented Essex from chasing a tricky target of 270 in four-and-three-quarter hours on a wicket that had helped the seam bowlers throughout. Then, in the final week of July, Worcestershire went down to successive defeats against Yorkshire at Scarborough and Hampshire at New Road. In both cases, Worcestershire were involved in unsuccessful run chases on the final afternoon, although both were in contrasting situations. At Scarborough, Yorkshire secured a 25-run lead on first innings, despite a masterly century from Tom Graveney, who received little support from his colleagues, and then towards the end of his innings, to make matters worse, he was also handicapped by a thigh strain. A brisk half-century by Phil Sharpe allowed Yorkshire to set Worcestershire a target of 207 in 140 minutes on the final afternoon. When Ron Headley was at the crease, a Worcestershire win looked a distinct possibility, but after his dismissal by Tony Nicholson, there was a flurry of wickets, and as the game entered the final hour, Kenyon's men tried to save the game. A dour rearguard action was mounted, but the spinners were starting to gain appreciable assistance, and Yorkshire duly secured a 92-run victory with just seven minutes remaining. The match against Hampshire at Worcester saw Kenyon's men chase a target of 315 on a pitch where only one batsman before the final day had passed fifty. That one was Henry Horton, the former Worcestershire batsman, who occupied the crease for almost four-and-a-half hours, making 79. Kenyon showed similar resolution as Worcestershire chased their target, but as in his side's first innings, there was a flurry of wickets against the new ball. First time around, Worcestershire had slipped to 15 for 3, and now in their run chase, they slumped to 12 for 3, before Kenyon, who had dropped down the order to number five, offered some stout resistance. But there was plenty of time for Hampshire's bowlers to steadily work away at the other end, and Worcestershire duly went down to their third defeat of the summer, by the comprehensive margin of 135 runs.

It proved to be Worcestershire's final reverse of the season, as their batsmen subsequently returned to form, none more so than Tom Graveney, who enjoyed a purple patch at the start of August, scoring three centuries in four Championship innings. His magnificent run began with 109 against Leicestershire at New Road, as he shared a match-winning partnership of 150 for the fifth wicket with Dick Richardson. It helped to secure a lead of 177, before Norman Gifford took 7/63 to finish with match figures of 10/87 as Worcestershire won by an innings and 27 runs. Graveney then scored 132 in the match at Worcester against Northamptonshire – his 100th first-class hundred – and an innings that helped Worcestershire secure a first-innings lead of 97 and the 2 bonus points they needed to go back to the top of the Championship table. But any thoughts of adding win points were scuppered, initially by a fightback by the visiting bowlers as Worcestershire were bundled out for 112 in their second innings, before rain swept in to prevent the visitors from getting near their target of 209, and the match ended in a draw.

Tom Graveney.

Graveney's third century, against Essex on a green wicket at Leyton, helped to trans-form Worcestershire's first innings, after Colin Hilton's new-ball spell had reduced them to 29 for 4. Graveney counterattacked with élan, and in four-and-a-half hours at the crease, he gave just one chance as he made 106. Essex's batsmen had few answers to the canny bowling of Flavell and Coldwall, and after Richardson had made an unbeaten 117, the two Worcester bowlers saw their side to a 167-run lead that con-solidated their position at the top of the Championship table.

Flavell was the match-winner again as Worcestershire visited Trent Bridge, but this time it was in the guise of tail-end batsman that the thirty-five year old saw his side home, as they chased 168 on the final afternoon. Having recorded match figures of 9/100, he must have had his feet up in the Nottingham pavilion, thinking that his day's work was over. But Worcestershire's second innings faltered and three cheap wickets fell as they slipped from 129 for 4 to 135 for 7. As Flavell strapped on his pads, a further 33 runs were needed, and this had become 9 when he was joined in the middle by last man Carter. The pressure was so great that some of the Worcestershire men went to the rear of the pavilion in an attempt to be oblivious to the drama out in the middle, while Graveney walked out to his vehicle in the car park, and to relieve the tension he sat there and attempted to finish a crossword. Out in the middle,

Roy Booth keeping wicket for Worcestershire at Swansea in May 1968, with Tom Graveney at slip, as Peter Walker plays a square cut.

Nottinghamshire's bowlers sensed a dramatic victory, but Flavell struck Keith Gillhouley for two boundaries to settle the match and keep his side on top of the county table.

Kenyon and his men then travelled down to Cheltenham to play Gloucestershire in the closing game of the famous festival at the college ground. The first game of the traditional festival had seen Warwickshire – Worcestershire's rivals at the top of the table – record a five-wicket victory, and then Glamorgan inflicted the second defeat on Ken Graveney's men as Gloucestershire were dismissed for just 55 in their second innings. Given this dip in Gloucestershire's form, many thought a Worcestershire win was a formality, and hundreds of Worcestershire supporters made their way to the Cotswold town. But they were in for something of a rude awakening as Worcestershire slipped to 39 for 5 as David Smith and Tony Brown made the ball lift and swing. Norman Gifford and Brian Brain swung lustily to see their side to 143, before Flavell and Brain had their turn to exploit the conditions and Gloucestershire were dismissed for an identical first-innings score. Batting appeared to be easier, as Worcestershire went to the crease again, with Kenyon making a fluent 91 and Headley a savage 66 as Gloucestershire's bowlers struggled to find any assistance in the conditions. Kenyon then set the home side a target of 282 in four-and-a-half hours, but apart from Ron Nicholls, there was little in the way of resistance from the Gloucestershire top order, as Flavell, Brain and Gifford, aided by some splendid fielding, worked their way through the batting. But there was more resistance from the tail, and when number eleven Ken Graveney walked out to the wicket, there were only thirty-five minutes left. As his brother spotted, 'Ken had that determined glint in his eye, and try as we did, we could not shift him. He batted as well then as I have ever seen him, and it was only the fact that we claimed the new ball, with four minutes to go, that finally sent him back. Flavell bowled one of his most hostile overs, and Ken was caught off his bat handle a minute from the end. We had run it very close, but another win – this time by 107 runs – was in the bag.'

The mood in the Worcester dressing room was lifted further as news came in from Edgbaston that Warwickshire had been bowled out by Derbyshire with just five minutes to spare, and the next morning, as Kenyon's men gathered at Kidderminster for the match against Middlesex, they proudly read in the daily newspapers of their handsome lead on top of the table.

Within a couple of hours, Flavell was making headlines all of his own, taking the first nine wickets to fall as Middlesex found batting well nigh impossible on a damp surface against the Worcestershire seamer. In fact, it might have been all ten had Anthony Waite not been dropped before he had scored. As the surface dried out, the Middlesex spinners then prevented Kenyon's men from mounting a handsome first-innings lead, as 9 wickets fell for just 24 runs. Run-scoring remained a difficult proposition as Middlesex batted for a second time, but with spirits high in the Worcester camp, their bowlers steadily worked their way through the Middlesex order, and then Kenyon joyously scored a brisk half-century to see his side to a decisive nine-wicket victory. This result also meant that Worcestershire would become County Champions if they recorded another victory in their following match against Gloucestershire at Worcester and Warwickshire failed to win against Hampshire at Southampton.

Roy Booth makes the stumping that secures the Championship

As the Worcestershire players gathered at New Road on 22 August for the match with Gloucestershire, they realised that they were on the verge of making history. Hundreds of gleeful supporters swarmed through the turnstiles at Worcester, eagerly hoping to see for themselves Worcestershire clinch their first ever Championship title. By the time the captains walked out to the middle to toss the coin, there was a buzz of expectation around the ground, and there must have been a few nerves jangling in the home team's dressing room after Worcestershire had elected to bat first. But Don Kenyon and Martin Horton quelled any feelings of anxiety by adding 187 for the first wicket, before Kenyon was bowled by John Mortimore for a fine 114. Horton soon followed as he was caught behind off Tony Windows just four short of a richly deserved hundred, but the momentum was maintained by a rollicking third-wicket partnership of 126 in 100 minutes between Headley and Graveney, and the West Indian reached his century shortly before Kenyon declared with Worcestershire on 398 for 3 – their highest total of the season. Weekend rain had freshened up the wicket when Gloucestershire batted on Monday morning, and to the delight of the home contingent, they were soon in trouble as Flavell took 3/9 in the space of 4 overs. Despite some late resistance from John Mortimore and Tony Windows, Gloucestershire followed-on 206 runs behind, and with news filtering through that Hampshire looked like gaining a first-innings lead over Warwickshire, Kenyon proudly led his side back onto the Worcester ground knowing that the Championship was at long last almost in their grasp. Flavell and Brain soon made early inroads as the Gloucestershire batsmen continued to struggle, and although David Allen launched a counterattack, Gifford's nagging spin meant that wickets fell at the other end. Allen eventually fell to the spinner for 68, and then after Brain had dismissed Windows, Gifford claimed the final and decisive wicket as Ken Graveney was deftly stumped by Roy Booth.

Worcestershire had won by an innings and two runs, so Kenyon led his triumphant team onto the balcony of the Worcester pavilion to receive a standing ovation from over a thousand spectators who, like the players themselves, were eagerly awaiting news from Southampton, where Hampshire had set Warwickshire a target of 314 at a rate of 90 runs an hour. With the Warwickshire run chase apparently going quite well, everyone had to patiently wait, with Kenyon and his team nervously gathering in the committee room with the club's officials, who had set up a special hotline to Southampton. At first, it looked as though Warwickshire's run-chase might succeed, as Bob Barber, Jim Stewart and Tom Cartwright all scored brisk half-centuries. But Hampshire's bowlers continued to pick up wickets, and many a fingernail was being bitten at Worcester as the game at Southampton entered the final quarter of an hour with Warwickshire needing 26 more runs and Hampshire 2 more wickets. To many, the wait seemed like a lifetime, but in fact, only an hour-and-three-quarters had elapsed since the end of the match at New Road when the phone call finally came through that everyone at Worcester had been waiting for – Derek Shackleton and 'Butch' White had polished off the Warwickshire tail, and Hampshire had won by 17 runs, and Worcestershire had won the Championship. Within a few seconds, the champagne corks were flying around the committee room, as Worcestershire proudly celebrated becoming County Champions for the first time in their history.

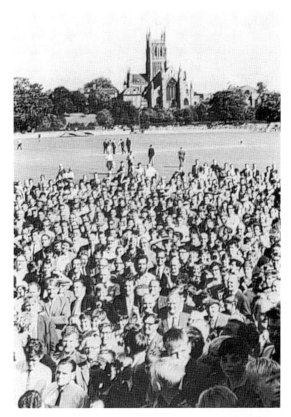

Right: A large crowd gathers in front of
the Worcester pavilion, eager for news
from Southampton.

Below: Don Kenyon and the
Worcestershire team celebrate in the
New Road dressing room after
confirmation of their Championship
success.

The County Championship Table for 1964

Pos.	County	Played	Won	Lost	Drawn	NR	Points
1	Worcestershire	28	18	3	6	1	191
2	Warwickshire	28	14	5	9	0	150
3	Northamptonshire	28	12	4	11	1	130
4	Surrey	28	11	3	13	1	129
5	Yorkshire	28	11	3	14	0	126
6	Middlesex	28	9	6	12	1	112
7	Kent	28	9	6	12	1	108
8	Somerset	28	8	8	8	4	96
9	Sussex	28	8	9	10	1	88
10	Essex	28	7	11	8	2	86
11	Glamorgan	28	7	7	12	2	84
12	Derbyshire	28	5	9	12	2	68
12	Hampshire	28	5	8	14	2	68
14	Lancashire	28	4	10	13	1	64
15	Nottinghamshire	28	4	13	11	0	54
16	Leicestershire	28	3	18	5	2	44
17	Gloucestershire	28	3	15	10	0	43

N.B.

The points totals for Surrey and Worcestershire include 1 point for a first-innings tie in a drawn match. The totals for Gloucestershire and Hampshire include 1 point for a first-innings tie in a lost match. The Hampshire total includes 5 points for a drawn match in which they were batting and scores finished level.

Sussex
The First 'One-Day Kings'

By the early 1960s there were other competitions, apart from the County Championship, in the summer calendar, following the introduction in 1963 of the Gillette Cup. The 65-over competition had been introduced by the game's administrators following concerns about dwindling attendances at county fixtures, and the dull nature of many games. The mandarins at Lord's hoped that the new form of instant, and exciting cricket would attract the crowds back to county cricket, and in its first year, the new knock-out competition saw Ted Dexter and his Sussex team defeat Worcestershire in the final at Lord's. Dexter's men duly retained the trophy in 1964 and it was only in their special challenge match on 14 September against the Australians at Hove that Sussex were eventually beaten in this form of cricket. Their winning run had embraced ten games, and among their scalps were the 1963 West Indians, who were defeated by four wickets in a 55-overs-a-side contest at Hove at the end of their tour.

May 1964 saw Sussex open their title defence by overwhelming Durham by 200 runs. Jim Parks struck an unbeaten 102 after Sussex had opted to bat first, despite the Hove ground being shrouded in a sea fret. Tony Buss then took four wickets as the visitors were dismissed for 93. The winning run continued in mid-June as Somerset were defeated at Taunton by 16 runs, but early in the match, it looked as if Bill Alley's side would turn the tables on Ted Dexter's team. Sussex slumped to 29 for 4, after Fred Rumsey and Geoff Hall had each taken two wickets in a lively opening burst. Graham Cooper then led a recovery, and his sober 58, made in two-and-a-half hours at the crease, guided his team to a more respectable position. But the target of 142 seemed a long way away as Sussex's bowlers also made early inroads, as the home team slipped to 27 for 4. But Roy Virgin was in obdurate mood, and as long as he was at the wicket, a Somerset victory seemed likely. But on 54 he was caught behind by Parks off Don Bates, and Somerset's resistance soon ended.

A month later a record crowd in excess of 15,000 crammed themselves into the compact Hove ground for the semi-final with Surrey. Sussex made a slow but steady start against Surrey's new-ball attack, before Dexter played a fine captain's innings, hitting a splendid 84 in two-and-a-half hours. Some late blows by Alan Oakman saw Sussex add 55 in the last 10 overs and set Surrey a target of 216. Surrey's top order then made a stuttering start against Sussex's battery of five seamers, and with Mickey Stewart and Ken Barrington both falling cheaply, the visitors never really got into their stride. Dexter also picked up three wickets as Surrey were dismissed for a mere 125, and after having taken two catches as well, few people disagreed with Frank Woolley's choice of Dexter as Man of the Match.

Left: Ted Dexter celebrates winning the Gillette Cup.

Below: The successful Sussex team – L.J. Lenham, N.I. Thomson, J.M. Parks, K.G. Suttle, D.L. Bates, E.R. Dexter, G.C. Cooper, R.J. Langridge, M.G. Griffith, A. Buss, J.A. Snow.

Opposite: Action from the 1964 Gillette Cup final, as Tom Cartwright is caught by Ted Dexter off the bowling of John Snow.

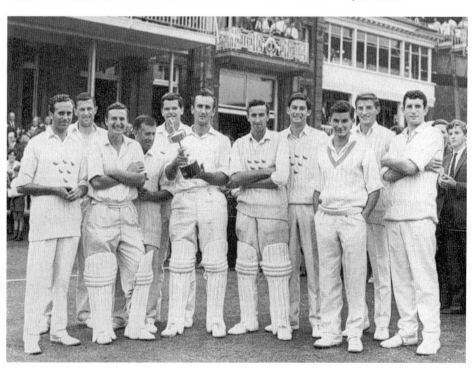

The final, against Warwickshire at Lord's, was another huge success for the Sussex seamers, especially Ian Thomson, whose 4/23 ripped the heart out of the opposition's batting. By lunch they had subsided to 61 for 6, and despite a valiant rearguard action by captain M.J.K. Smith, plus wicketkeeper A.C. Smith, Warwickshire were never able to break free from the stranglehold that Thomson had exerted, and were dismissed in the forty-eighth over for a paltry 127. There were few gremlins in the wicket as Les Lenham and Ken Suttle began Sussex's reply and the pair shared an opening stand of 92 in 31 overs. Even though both fell in quick succession, their partnership had settled the outcome, and well before the sun had started to set, Dexter's men and their band of loyal supporters were celebrating their second success in a Lord's final.

Not everyone, though, was delighted with the way that Sussex played their one-day games. Some commentators accused Dexter's team of playing negative cricket, and setting defensive fields to stifle run-scoring. Their detractors argued instead that the creation of the limited-overs games had been to stimulate bright and breezy cricket, with plenty of attractive and dashing strokeplay. But Dexter and his team thought otherwise, believing that the key to success in this new form of the game was to employ defensive fields and defy the opposition to break through. Many other captains set conventional fields, as if the match were the opening day of a Championship contest, but they paid the ultimate price as more and more counties realised that the new form of the game required a new mindset, with tight aggressive bowling and defensive field placings. Ted Dexter had stolen a march on his rival captains, and as he later wrote in his autobiography, 'we won the first two Gillette Cups before the other counties had woken up to the issues that these one-day games brought. I remember the first game against Kent at Tunbridge Wells. We won the toss and Colin Cowdrey set a very friendly field indeed.

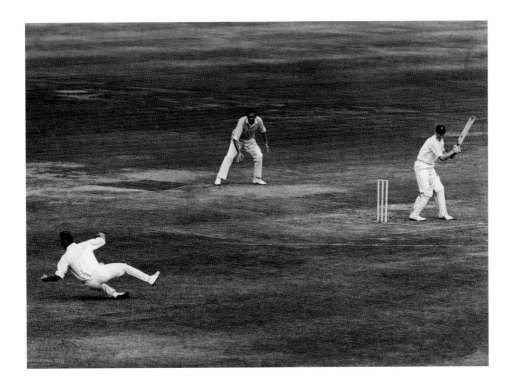

Ted Dexter bowling for the Gentlemen against the Players at Lord's in July, 1962. John Edrich is the non-striker and Ossie Wheatley is the fielder.

Ted Dexter, and Man of the Match Ian Thomson, with the 1964 Gillette Cup.

We made a big score; it was all very sporting and pleased the big crowd. Then Kent went in and the picture changed dramatically. There was only one man who looked like doing any good and that was Peter Richardson. It was not my intention to get him out – I just set the field back, allowed him to take a single, then bowled tight to the other batsmen to force him to make the runs and not Richardson. There were boos and screams and everyone thought this was a rotten thing to do – but there it was, for I had shown people what they could be let in for with one-day cricket.'

Gillette Cup Final 1964

Sussex *v.* Warwickshire
Lord's
5 September 1964

Result: Sussex won by eight wickets
Toss: Warwickshire
Umpires: A.E. Fagg and A.E.G. Rhodes
Man of the Match: N.I. Thomson

Warwickshire innings

N.F. Horner	b Thomson		12
R.W. Barber	c Parks	b Thomson	3
K. Ibadulla		b Thomson	2
*M.J.K. Smith		b Snow	28
W.J.P. Stewart	c Parks	b Buss	17
J.A. Jameson		b Thomson	4
T.W. Cartwright	c Dexter	b Snow	7
R.E. Hitchcock	c Parks	b Dexter	8
+A.C. Smith	not out		35
J.D. Bannister	c Parks	b Dexter	0
D.J. Brown	c Suttle	b Dexter	0
Extras	(b 1, lb 9, nb 1)		11
Total	(all out, 48 overs)		127

FoW: 1-9, 2-18, 3-21, 4-52, 5-61,
6-81, 7-84, 8-111, 9-113

Bowling	O	M	R	W
Thomson	13	5	23	4
Buss	11	0	30	1
Snow	12	1	28	2
Bates	7	0	29	0
Dexter	5	3	6	3

Sussex innings

K.G. Suttle	c M.J.K. Smith	b Ibadulla	42
L.J. Lenham		b Cartwright	47
*E.R. Dexter		not out	17
+J.M. Parks		not out	21
G.C. Cooper			
R.J. Langridge			
M.G. Griffith			
N.I. Thomson			
A. Buss			
J.A. Snow			
D.L. Bates			
Extras	(lb 3, nb 1)		4
Total	(for 2 wickets, 41.2 overs)		131

FoW: 1-92, 2-97

Bowling	O	M	R	W
Brown	6	3	15	0
Bannister	13	2	46	0
Cartwright	12	1	30	1
Ibadulla	10	2	28	1
M.J.K. Smith	0.2	0	8	0

A Season to Savour

At 2.40 p.m. during the Fifth Test at The Oval on 15 August 1964, Fred Trueman became the first bowler in cricket history to reach 300 wickets in Test cricket, as Australia's Neil Hawke edged a ball from the Yorkshire paceman into the hands of Colin Cowdrey at slip. It crowned a joyous return to the England side for both Trueman and Cowdrey, whom the selectors had omitted for the previous Test at Old Trafford. Fred had arrived at The Oval still needing three victims to become the first Englishman to take 300 wickets, but after the first few days of the match, and with the Australian batsmen going well, it looked as if he would leave The Oval still three short of the landmark. On the Friday evening, Fred had trudged off with figures of 0/55 as Australia reached 245 for 5 at the close, and then the following morning, Ian Redpath and Wally Grout lashed Fred for a further 25 runs in 5 overs. However, the Yorkshire paceman was still eager to have another crack at the Aussies, so when captain Ted Dexter was mulling over his bowling options shortly before lunch, Fred walked up to him and said 'Here, give us the cherry!'

'Right, but bowl off your short run, Fred' replied the England captain, and to his delight Fred then knocked back Ian Redpath's middle stump with his fifth delivery. With the next, an away-swinger, Graham McKenzie snicked the ball into Cowdrey's hands in the slips, and Fred walked off for lunch and went into The Oval pavilion on 299 victims. Just to add spice to things he was also on a hat-trick. As he later wrote in *The Freddie Trueman Story*, the forty minutes of the lunch break were some of the longest of his life. 'I've forgotten what was for lunch or even whether I ate it. Everything was a kind of dream. People had said I had a flair for the big occasion, but this is ridiculous. I had been stuck on 297 wickets for so long that I thought the magic 300 would never come. Now fate was ready to hand me the prize with a hat-trick thrown in!

'The hat-trick never happened. That fateful first delivery after lunch passed Neil Hawke's off stump and wrecked that idea. Half an hour went by and I started wondering whether fate would leave me poised forever on that tantalising 299. Then I took the new ball. Neil Hawke got a thick edge and Colin snapped it up by his right knee.

'I stood in the middle of the pitch and raised my hands to heaven as the applause crashed out. Hawke was the first to reach me and shake my hand, then all of my England buddies followed. I grabbed Colin and hugged him unashamedly. I was so overcome I didn't know whether to laugh or cry.'

1964 was also a good year for another famous Yorkshire cricketer – Geoff Boycott. On 4 June, the man who was destined to become one of England's greatest opening

This page, clockwise from top:

Fred Trueman and other members of the England team, training on board ship en route to Australia, spurred on by athlete Gordon Pirie (wearing white shorts).

Fred Trueman leaves the field at The Oval after taking his 300th Test wicket.

'Fiery Fred' in his delivery stride.

Opposite page, left: Geoff Boycott (left) going out to bat with Ken Taylor for Yorkshire at Scarborough.

Opposite page, right: John Edrich.

batsmen of the modern era played in his first ever Test match, against Australia at Nottingham. Then, in the Fifth Test at The Oval 'Sir Geoffrey' recorded his maiden hundred for England, making 113 in England's second innings.

Right from an early age one of Geoffrey's ambitions had been to play for England and, for the bespectacled young man who had only a few years before taken a temporary job as a clerical assistant with the Yorkshire Electricity Board in Wakefield, his dream came true in the opening Test of the Ashes series at Trent Bridge. The previous year he had enjoyed a wonderful year for Yorkshire, and the opener had been voted by the Cricket Writers' Club as the 'Young Cricketer of the Year'. With his star in the ascendancy, he was included, at the end of May 1964, in the MCC side to play the Australians at Lord's. In true Boycott style, he responded with a steady 63 and shared an opening stand of 124 with Brian Bolus that occupied over half of the day's play. While Michael Melford, the highly respected and influential cricket correspondent of *The Daily Telegraph* described their opening stand as turgid, he also recognised Boycott's potential against the Test bowlers. 'During much of their opening stand Boycott and Bolus played with fair comfort, even if their timing was not perfect,' Melford wrote, 'and on this slow outfield, they were unable to rise much above two runs an over. There were times in the early afternoon when Boycott's innings in particular promised to bloom into something attractive, but Hawke and Veivers bowled a useful containing spell. Boycott's zest for making runs was apparent, as were his confidence and watchfulness, but though his timing improved a little after lunch, he was still not able to thrust home the advantage.'

In his heart, Boycott felt that he hadn't quite done enough playing for the MCC to force his claim to a Test place, but aware of his decent form in the Championship, the selectors decided to give him a go, choosing the Yorkshireman to open the innings with Surrey left-hander John Edrich. But England's preparations for the opening

match of the Ashes series were then disrupted by something of a freak injury to Edrich, who the day before trod on a ball while practising and twisted his ankle. The swelling had not gone down the following morning, so an hour before play was due to start, Edrich was declared unfit and Fred Titmus, the Middlesex off-spinner, was promoted to open the innings with Boycott.

Soon afterwards, Ted Dexter won the toss, and the somewhat unlikely, and untried, combination of Boycott and Titmus walked out from the famous Nottingham pavilion to begin England's innings. As Boycott later wrote in his autobiography, 'The whole Test scene was fascinatingly new, not totally intimidating, but unexplored and unfolding... I remember being nervous at first, so nervous that I picked up my bat to play the opening delivery from Graham McKenzie and it was in Grout's gloves before I had time to play a shot! McKenzie chipped a bone in my finger and I couldn't bat in the second innings, but I made 48, top score in the first innings, before being caught by Bobby Simpson off Grahame Corling.'

The finger injury forced Boycott to miss the Second Test at Lord's, but rather than select another opener Dexter was promoted up the order and, after proving his fitness with Yorkshire, Boycott returned on his home ground Headingley for the Third Test, where his parents proudly watched him resume his Test career. In the following Test at Old Trafford, Boycott scored his first half-century for England, and then in the second week of August, after hearing confirmation that he was in the MCC party for the winter tour to South Africa, Boycott celebrated with a fine 122 for Yorkshire against the tourists at Bradford. The news of his selection for the winter tour really lifted his

Left: Geoff Boycott strikes another boundary on the off side.

Opposite: Ken Barrington in aggressive batting mood, pulling a ball to the boundary in Surrey's match against Middlesex at The Oval in 1965, watched by wicketkeeper John Murray, and slip fielders Peter Parfitt (left) and Fred Titmus.

morale, as there had been moments during the Test series when he had started to won-
der whether he was good enough to play at Test level. After being dismissed several
times by Corling, he slightly modified his technique, and as his subsequent innings
proved, this self-analysis and willingness to adapt paid off. His century against the full
Australian Test attack at Bradford meant that Boycott entered the final Test with his
spirits high, and in the second innings, he crowned a memorable summer with his
maiden Test hundred. England were 197 runs behind when Boycott and his new opening partner Bob Barber began the innings. With two-and-a-half days remaining, an
Australian victory was still a possibility, but The Oval wicket was easy paced, and with
Boycott and Barber adopting a positive outlook, they launched the innings by adding
80 for the first wicket. Despite the later loss of Dexter for 24, Boycott then found a
useful ally in Fred Titmus, as the Middlesex man was promoted up the order again, this
time as nightwatchman. Titmus hung around for three-and-a-half hours, and with the
other end secure, Boycott started to unfurl some fine drives and fierce cuts square of
the wicket. After around five hours at the crease, Boycott made it to three figures,
with his trademark shot, forcing the ball through the covers off the back foot – his
ninth boundary – before falling to Bobby Simpson's gentle leg-breaks for 113. Colin
Cowdrey and Ken Barrington then took advantage of the tiring Australian attack, and
by the end of the day's play, England were 184 runs ahead. Rain on the final day dashed
England's hopes of setting the Aussies a challenging target, and the match was drawn.
There may not have been a positive outlook, but at least the match had seen the arrival
on the international stage of Geoffrey Boycott.

1964 was Ken Barrington's Benefit year, and the Surrey and England batsman celebrated by being England's leading run-scorer in the Ashes series, as well as heading the domestic batting averages with his seasonal aggregate standing at 1,872 runs at an average of 62.40. Barrington enjoyed a purple patch in the final week of July, and the first few days of August, during which he recorded two double-hundreds – 207 for Surrey against Nottinghamshire at The Oval, and 256 for England in the Fourth Test against Australia at Old Trafford. The latter was also his first Test century on English soil, and it had irked him that prior to the 1964 summer, his previous 9 hundreds for England had been scored overseas. For someone who was a fine back-foot player, it was no surprise that he should have prospered in Test Matches in Australia and the West Indies, where the hard, bouncy wickets assisted his strengths. But it still irritated him that he had yet to score a Test hundred in England and at the start of the 1964 Ashes series Barrington was determined to set the record straight and reach three figures at home. At Headingley in England's second innings of the Third Test, Barrington looked as if he would reach this personal milestone, but as he went on past 50, he started to become more cautious, and as he stopped making shots, Bobby Simpson brought in the field and crowded Barrington. The Surrey man was on 85 when he padded up to a ball from Tom Veivers that he believed pitched outside off stump. Umpire Fred Price thought otherwise and upheld the Aussies' appeal, so Barrington trudged back to the pavilion having failed to score the elusive hundred at home.

Barrington felt that the situation called for drastic measures so, as he wrote in his autobiography *Playing it Straight*, he resorted to superstition. 'Before the Fourth Test at Old Trafford, I did three things. For the first time in nine years, I took Peter May's lucky half-crown from my England blazer and left it on a shelf in the kitchen before I drove to Manchester. Having got there purposely two hours before reporting time, I almost literally dived for my favourite corner of the dressing room. Thirdly, I asked my wife Ann to change the wording of the telegram she always sent me on the first morning of a home Test and which I traditionally carry in the hip pocket of my flannels throughout the game. The telegram duly arrived – "*Vincit qui patitur* – Love Ann" but not having learnt Latin at school, I hadn't a clue what it meant, but at least Ann had sent something different.'

Australia then rattled up 656 for 8, as Bobby Simpson believed that being one up and with two Tests still to play, he should steer his side into a position where his team could not lose. Simpson's contribution was 311 in twelve-and-three-quarter hours, and when he declared at 12.30 p.m. on the third day, it meant that England needed the small measure of 457 to avoid the follow-on. For three hours, Barrington waited in the pavilion, but then with the score on 126, Boycott was bowled. 'I walked to the middle for my forty-fifth Test innings in England,' he later recalled, 'with 331 still wanted to save the follow on! I vowed I wouldn't even attempt a forcing stroke until I felt in. It was a terribly frustrating feeling; the need to bat and bat with no hope of winning, and the tension in front of 30,000 people made me more edgy than usual.'

But Barrington carefully played himself in, and with Dexter in good form, the pair proceeded to add 246 for the third wicket. But it wasn't all plain sailing, as Dexter survived a couple of sharp chances to Graham McKenzie, and when Barrington went into his shell against Veivers, Simpson brought up four short legs. But after his disappointments at Manchester, Barrington was even more determined to get it right and, slowly but surely, he entered the nineties. As he later wrote, 'After looking up at the scoreboard and realising I was within striking distance of the "ton", I wrestled with my own impatience and excitement – "wait, wait" I muttered to myself; it will come, wait for the odd bad ball! I stuck, as though immobilised and run-less forever at one stage, but at last, I crawled through those nineties to 99. Straight ball, straight ball, straight ball, and then Veivers delivered one outside the off stump. In a split second I saw it as the chance to play my favourite dab for one.

'I went for the shot; realised too late that the ball was farther up than I'd thought and had gained a bit of bounce off the pitch. I got a hard top edge. It flew hard and slightly to the right of McKenzie at short slip. I saw his hand grasp at it and then a terrific roar from the crowd… and a split second later the sight of the ball being chased… the heady sensation of scampering for two runs and seeing my figures on the scoreboard: 101.'

As the applause died down, Barrington realised that although his personal milestone had been reached, his job for the side was still not over, so he got his head down, and set his sights on a second hundred. Despite being hit on the left shoulder by Graham Corling, and having treatment on the field, Barrington made it to 200, and when he was finally dismissed for 256, he had batted for a fraction under eleven-and-a-half hours. It was a very satisfied Barrington who returned to the pavilion: with England's total on 594 for 7, he had helped them avoid the follow on, and moreover, he had finally scored a Test hundred in England. 'As the congratulatory cables began to arrive, I pulled Ann's telegram from my flannel pocket. The changed message had certainly done its stuff. When I got home to Mitcham, she told me what it meant: "vincit qui patitur – he who endures, conquers".'

1964 was the sixth time that Ray Illingworth, the Yorkshire batsman and off spinner did the Double. The thirty-two year old had previously achieved the feat in 1957, 1959, 1960, 1961 and 1962, and his aggregate of 1,301 runs and 122 wickets in 1964 saw him to the coveted landmark again. However, 1964 was the final time in his illustrious career that 'Illy' achieved the feat of 1,000 runs and 100 wickets in first-class cricket, although this was not as a result of a decline in his abilities as a cricketer. Far from it, as he remained one of England's best spinners, and someone who could also still play a match-winning innings. But as he became a senior player in the Yorkshire side, there were other things on his mind, and although keeping a wary eye on the averages, he often put the team before any personal glory. As Fred Trueman once put it, 'if Raymond had played with any other county he'd have gone in number three or four and got 2,000 runs easy. Playing with Yorkshire, many a time he had to throw his wicket away. To give him credit, he was never loath to do it for his side.' In fact, his readiness to hit the ball in the air when the situation demanded it brought Illingworth the nickname of 'Slam-Slam' among his dressing-room colleagues in the early 1960s, but even they would have agreed that 'Illy' had a fine technique, was quick into line, a brave player of fast bowling, and perhaps above all else, someone who knew exactly where his off stump lay. Evidence of Illingworth's fine technique and willingness to put bat to ball came in Yorkshire's match in mid-August against Kent at Dover where he scored 135 and returned match figures of 14/101. It was his only Championship century of the summer, and it was achieved on a damp Dover wicket where the next highest score in the match was a mere 36. Whereas every other batsman struggled on the wet surface, 'Illy' drove the ball cleanly, striking 15 fours and 1 six, as Yorkshire reached 256, and then dismissed Kent twice on the second day, with Illingworth taking 7 wickets in each innings.

Illingworth did not feature in the 1964 Ashes series as the selectors gave preference to John Mortimore as Fred Titmus' spinning partner. Titmus was widely regarded as England's number one off-spinner, although Jimmie Binks, the Yorkshire wicketkeeper thought otherwise. 'Raymond was the best off spinner I played with or against. He was one of the hardest to keep to as well, as the variations of his flight were so subtle. He bowled such a good out-swinger and when he wanted to be he was a yard quicker than most.'

These were attributes that, although overlooked by the English selectors in 1964, were put to good use for Yorkshire, for whom he took 104 Championship wickets. On several occasions, he produced some decisive second-innings spells, and in addition to his fine figures at Dover, his 6/50 at Headingley saw Yorkshire inflict a ten-wicket defeat on Middlesex, while his 7/89 against Nottinghamshire saw his team record an eight-wicket victory at Scarborough.

Ian Thomson was a fine swing bowler and, as he proved twice in 1964, if the conditions were in his favour, the Sussex man could be almost unplayable. The tall seamer had a rather ordinary approach to the wicket, in fact it was described by some observers as more like a shuffle than a run-up, but in his delivery stride he fully extended his six-foot frame, and with his high action he extracted any lift that lay in the surface. Thomson's stock ball was an in-swinger that often moved late into the batsman, but he also possessed one that swung the other way, and it was this leg-cutter as well as the off-cutter that, in the right conditions, made Thomson so much of a handful as batsmen were unsure of which way the ball was going. At Worthing on 6 June 1964, Thomson used these attributes to become only the eighth bowler since the Second World War to take all ten wickets in an innings in a Championship match. His figures of 10/49 against Warwickshire also saw him become the first Sussex bowler for sixty-five years to take all ten, yet despite his ruthless exploitation of the rain-affected wicket, he ended up on the losing side as Sussex were bustled out in the space of just fifty-five minutes for 23 in their second innings, as Warwickshire won a remarkable match by 182 runs. Then on the first Saturday in September, in the Gillette Cup final against Warwickshire, Thomson produced a bewildering spell of swing bowling from the Pavilion End that effectively decided the outcome of the contest. Thomson's figures of 4/23 earned the bowler the Man of the Match award as Sussex retained the one-day trophy. In his opening 8 overs, Thomson took 4/17 and he made the ball swing in a disconcerting manner in the hazy atmosphere, leaving Mike Smith, the Warwickshire captain, reflecting on whether or not he should have elected to bat first after winning the toss. Although his side recovered to make 127, it was never going to be enough against Ted Dexter and the rest of the Sussex batsmen who were so adept at the one-day game. These performances during 1964 were a worthy reward for a man who for twelve successive seasons claimed over 100 wickets, and by the time he played his last game, in the 1972 season, he had 1,597 wickets to his name, at an average of 20.58. A record that fully justified the claim that Thomson was the best right-arm seam bowler produced by the South Coast county since the legendary Maurice Tate.

Ian Thomson.   Ray Illingworth.

Arnold Long, the twenty-three year old Surrey wicketkeeper, had a couple of days to remember in mid-July 1964 as he equalled several English wicketkeeping records during the Championship match against Sussex at Hove. With the Surrey seamers exploiting a green-tinted Hove wicket, Long equalled the domestic record by holding seven catches in Sussex's first innings. Then when Sussex batted again, he added three more victims, before pouching an edge from Francis Pountain to take his match aggregate to eleven, one behind the English record of twelve set by Ted Pooley, coincidentally in Surrey's match against Sussex at The Oval in 1868. There were 3 wickets still to fall, and with the wicket continuing to behave capriciously, there was every chance that 'Ob' Long might equal Pooley's feats. But Ian Thomson was then well held by Barrington in the slips, before Bell edged to Storey to give David Sydenham his eleventh wicket of the match. With Sussex's last pair at the wicket, Long had a final chance to equal the English record, and when Alan Oakman flailed at a ball from Stewart Storey, Long made a desperate attempt to catch hold of the thick edge. But the ball flew to Ken Barrington at first slip, and the England batsman made no mistake by holding onto the ball. Nevertheless, Long received a standing ovation from the Sussex crowd, although the Surrey gloveman was blissfully unaware of how close he was to rewriting cricket history. 'I had no idea that I was so close to the world record,' he later said, 'but I thought I must have been near it. It was certainly a great feeling to hold that catch from Pountain, and I have never been so thrilled since I first kept wicket at school.'

John Murray, of Middlesex and England, was another wicketkeeper to enjoy a fine summer in 1964, but this time it was as a batsman with the twenty-nine year old scoring 1,000 runs for the fourth time in his career to remind the England selectors,

Clockwise from top:

Arnold Long catches an edge from Peter Walker's bat in Surrey's match against Glamorgan at The Oval in September 1971. Graham Roope and Stewart Storey are the happy Surrey fielders.

John Murray.

John Murray keeping wicket, as fellow wicketkeeper Alan Knott edges a ball past the outstretched hands of Peter Parfitt in Middlesex's match against Kent at Lord's in May 1969.

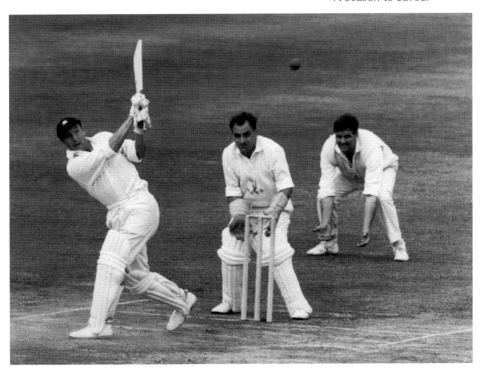

John Murray hits to leg in Middlesex's match against Glamorgan at Lord's in 1965. David Evans is the wicketkeeper, while Jim Pressdee is at slip.

who had overlooked him for the Test series, that he was a fine batsman as well as something of a perfectionist as a wicketkeeper. 'J.T.' was a great technician behind the stumps, always showing excellent positioning and balance, coupled with great agility. He rarely missed any chance that was remotely within his diving range when standing back to the Middlesex seamers. Just to add to the air of excellence, Murray was always immaculately turned out, and was elegance personified even when taking the ball, and throwing it to the slip fielders standing alongside him. He was also a fine batsman, with an exquisite drive, both on the on and off side, as well as being a fearless hooker of anything dropped short – attributes that were to the fore in 1966 when he struck a hundred against the West Indies at The Oval, unfurling such classical strokes off the front foot that his partner Tom Graveney would have been proud of playing them. Injuries in India in 1961/62 and then in Australia in 1962/63 had seen Murray lose the England place he had first won back in the 1961 Ashes series. So while Sussex's Jim Parks was the selectors' choice for the 1964 rubber against the Australians, largely in order to strengthen the batting, Murray maintained an exceptionally high standard of keeping for Middlesex, as well as reminding the selectors of his batting ability. In all, Murray struck 1,040 Championship runs during 1964, including an unbeaten 111 against Yorkshire at Headingley, during a seventh-wicket partnership of 220 – at the time a record against Yorkshire – with Don Bennett that temporarily wrested the initiative back from the Yorkshire bowlers.

Mike Brearley OBE, who went on to captain England between 1977 and 1982, and win 39 Test caps, was voted by the Cricket Writer's Club as the Young Cricketer of the

Year for 1964. It followed a memorable summer for the young Middlesex batsman who completed his studies in Classics and Moral Sciences at Cambridge. During his time in residence at St John's College, Brearley had won four cricket Blues, and amassed an aggregate of 4,348 runs – a record for a university career. His studies at Cambridge meant that he did not play for Middlesex until the second half of the summer, but after coming down, he made an immediate impact and a number of astute judges noted his name as a future England player. In particular, he struck an unbeaten 106 in three-and-a-half hours in the second innings of Middlesex's match against the Australians, and although the tourists used their occasional bowlers towards the end of his innings, his earlier driving and cutting against the main bowlers had impressed several of the watching journalists and former players in the Lord's press box. One of these was Sir Frank Worrell, the great West Indian, who wrote 'young Mike Brearley batted on this wicket with the confidence one would expect from him at Fenner's. He has shown his ability to readjust himself to conditions and, but for an uncertain period against Australian leg spinner Rex Sellers, seemed to have plenty of time to make his shots. It was a highly intelligent exhibition for Middlesex of selection strokeplay. He has the temperament for the job of an opener which will serve him in good stead if, or when, he finds himself in a Test match environment.'

The second half of the summer saw a number of honours coming Brearley's way. He was awarded his Middlesex cap, while his outstanding captaincy at Cambridge, where he had led the XI with great aplomb and tactical acumen in 1962 and 1963, was recognised with his selection as leader of the President of the MCC's XI against the Australians in mid-August at Lord's. His team was full of up-and-coming English cricketers, and he produced the MCC's top score of the match with a mature 67 in their second innings. It really was a season to savour for Brearley, as he finished the year with 2,178 first-class runs to his name, which included 4 centuries for Cambridge, as well as his ton for Middlesex against the tourists. His reward was a place on the MCC winter tour to South Africa, with some predicting that he might make his Test debut in the Cape. However, he met with less success there, and it was not until 1976, and then after a brief sojourn away from cricket in the world of academia in the UK and North America, that Brearley eventually won his first Test cap. But the tour to South Africa in the winter of 1964/65 did provide him with an opportunity to taste the atmosphere of international cricket as he acted at times as the England twelfth man. However, as he later wrote in *The Art of Captaincy*, there were other things on his mind at the time – 'I acted as twelfth man while England batted in the Test in Johannesburg. Bob Barber and I happened to be in the middle of a chess game. When he called me onto the field during his innings, ostensibly for some dry gloves, his purpose was to inform me that his next move was queen's pawn to QB4 !' Such a situation was no real surprise, as Brearley was one of the most cerebral cricketers of the recent past, and he could hold as equally intelligent a conversation about the writings of Brecht or the compositions of Beethoven, as he could about the batting technique of Bradman.

Don Shepherd was another player to have very fond memories of the summer of '64. In addition to being a member of the first Glamorgan side to defeat the Australians, 'Shep' took the first and only hat-trick of his county career. This is a remarkable statistic given the fact that during his magnificent career, Shepherd took 2,174 first-class wickets for the Welsh county. But the off-cutter's career was full of

Clockwise from top left:

Mike Brearley.

Micky Norman.

The Cambridge University side of 1964: From left to right, standing: M.G. Griffith, I.G. Thwaites, D.M. Daniels, A.A. McLachlan, G.C. Pritchard, M.H. Rose. Sitting: R.C. White, R.C. Kerslake, J.M. Brearley, R.A. Hutton, A.R. Windows.

intriguing statistics, none more so perhaps than that he took more wickets than any other bowler who never won Test honours for England. Shepherd made his Glamorgan debut in 1950, and like many other great spinners, he started his career as a lively seam bowler. He changed styles in the mid-1950s and until the early 1970s he was the bulwark of the Glamorgan attack, relishing the task of tricking and teasing opposing batsmen with his vast armoury of deliveries, and almost despising anyone who freely took runs off him. Swansea was Shepherd's home patch, as it was here, on the dry and sandy wickets, that he produced some of his finest performances, and all within a few miles of the Gower Peninsula where he had grown up and played his first game of cricket. It was therefore very appropriate that 'Shep' should record his first county hat-trick at the St Helen's ground in mid-June 1964 as Glamorgan defeated Northamptonshire by seven wickets. The visitors had struggled after deciding to bat first, but by mid-afternoon, they were all out for 98 as Shepherd and Jim Pressdee shared nine wickets between them. Glamorgan's openers, Alan Jones and Bernard Hedges, then cleared off the arrears before being separated, but the innings then went into sharp decline as Jim Watts took 5/25. Starting 84 runs behind, the visiting batsmen fared slightly better second time around, but wickets continued to fall against the Glamorgan bowlers, and with Northants on 132 for 5, 'Shep' took his hat-trick. Firstly, Albert Lightfoot edged a ball from the off-cutter into the hands of Peter Walker at bad-pad, then Malcolm Scott got a faint edge to his first delivery and was caught behind by wicketkeeper David Evans. To the next ball, Brian Crump edged to Walker and the delighted Glamorgan team thronged around Shepherd to offer the great bowler their warmest congratulations.

While Don Shepherd could look back with pride about his efforts in the match with Northants at Swansea in mid-June 1964, Micky Norman, the visitors' opening batsman would rather forget the events of the first day, as on 10 June the thirty-one-year-old achieved the rather unenviable distinction of being dismissed first ball twice in the day. Whereas his colleagues were largely tricked and teased by the Glamorgan spinners, it was the clever pace bowling of Ossie Wheatley that proved to be the undoing of the Northants opener, as the Glamorgan seamer struck with his first delivery of each innings. The day began with Norman fending off a lifter from Wheatley into the hands of Peter Walker at short leg, and then later in the afternoon, as his team batted again, he edged the first ball of the second innings from Wheatley straight into the hands of Jim Pressdee in the slips. As the Glamorgan fielders congratulated their captain for striking again with the first ball of his spell, the fair-haired Northants batsman had to trudge back up the long flight of steps to the Swansea pavilion, for the second time in the day, not quite believing his ill fortune in having recorded a 'king pair' within the space of six hours' play.

The Counties in 1964

1964 saw Worcestershire's dream of the county title become a reality, yet for a while it looked as if Warwickshire were on course to become the first-ever county side to achieve the double of winning the County Championship and the Gillette Cup. At the end of the day, they won neither, and despite heading the Championship table for much of the season, the Edgbaston club ended up in second place behind their Midland neighbours.

Despite the best efforts of captain M.J.K. Smith, Warwickshire only won one of their last five matches of the summer. Their collective loss of form was rather disappointing, especially given the fact that at the start of August, Warwickshire had defeated the Australian tourists by 9 runs in a fine match at Edgbaston. Tom Cartwright was the county's most successful bowler in 1964. The twenty-nine year old from Coventry was the epitome of accuracy, and he finished a good summer with the handsome return of 128 championship wickets, each costing a fraction under 14 runs. Few county batsmen were able to take liberties against the medium-pacer, and two of Warwickshire's home games in June 1964 bore testament to Cartwright's metronomic bowling skills. Firstly at Nuneaton, Cartwight returned the match figures of 9/40 from 28.2 overs as Nottinghamshire were dismissed for just 34 and 57, with Warwickshire recording an innings victory and completely outclassing their opponents from the East Midlands. The following week, Cartwright's prowess with the ball saw Warwickshire defeat Kent at Edgbaston by 109 runs. The visitors never looked like scoring 260 on the final afternoon, as Cartwright returned figures of 27-11-56-7, with his last five victims coming in the space of 7 overs and at a cost of just 8 runs. Cartwright's efforts were rewarded with a place in the England side for the Fourth and Fifth Tests against Australia, but although very proud of making his Test debut at Old Trafford, how the Warwickshire man must have wished that his county side had been able to maintain their form from the first part of the summer and secure the Championship title.

While Warwickshire tailed off at the end of the season, Northamptonshire enjoyed a strong late run, and Keith Andrew's side finished in a highly creditable third place. In fact, they might have even mounted a serious challenge to Worcestershire had it not been for a damp and dreary spell between mid-May and mid-June that saw the East Midlands club secure just 2 points from 7 games. The second half of the season saw Northants record 8 victories, and only on two previous occasions – 1912 and 1957 – had the county finished in a higher position in the table. Roger Prideaux enjoyed a fine season, amassing 1,637 runs in his forty-seven Championship innings. Two other

Clockwise from top left:

Mike Smith is caught by Tom Graveney off Martin Horton's bowling in Worcestershire's match against Warwickshire at Edgbaston. Roy Booth is the wicketkeeper.

Tom Cartwright.

Colin Milburn (right) going out to bat at the Scarborough Festival with Gordon Barker.

Keith Andrew.

batsmen passed the thousand mark – Brian Reynolds and Colin Milburn, the twenty-two year old from County Durham Milburn's ebullient strokeplay was one of the features of the summer for Northants supporters, and together with Reynolds, he shared an opening stand of 176 in just two-and-a-half hours against Warwickshire at the Wantage Road ground. Milburn's share was 117 with twenty powerfully struck boundaries, and his free scoring was in stark contrast to Reynolds, who occupied the crease for over five hours in scoring 112, and for no less than forty-three minutes seemed marooned on 99, before finally reaching his second hundred of the summer. In mid-August, the cheerful Geordie followed this up with another quick-fire hundred at Northampton, making 104 against Middlesex. His aggressive and thrilling strokeplay continued to decorate the county game throughout the 1960s, and it was because of innings like these in 1964 that for the many devotees of Championship cricket, 'Ollie' Milburn was one of their favourite sons.

Surrey had been among the most successful of county teams during the 1950s, with the 'brown-hatters' winning the title on seven occasions. The 1960s saw a phase of rebuilding and with Surrey losing the services of Tony Lock and Peter Loader prior to the 1964 season, few people expected the South London club to have the firepower to mount a serious challenge for the title. As it turned out, Micky Stewart's side were never in serious contention for the Championship, but even so, they rose up from eleventh place to fourth – a very worthy effort and all largely without the services of experienced batsmen Ken Barrington and John Edrich, who played in five and four of the Ashes Tests respectively. In their absence, Stewart enjoyed a highly productive summer, amassing 1,792 runs in Championship matches, and scoring six hundreds – five of which were at The Oval, including an unbeaten 227 against Middlesex. 1964 was Stewart's second year at the helm, and after a modest baptism, he took great delight in steering Surrey to eleven Championship successes, in addition to a fine run in the Gillette Cup. Victories over Cheshire, Gloucestershire and Middlesex – the latter by 146 runs – saw Stewart's team to the semi-final of the 65-overs competition and a game at Hove against Sussex in front of what at the time was a record crowd of 15,000. It proved though to be something of an anticlimax for the Surrey side, who chasing 216 to win, were dismissed for a mere 125 with Stewart failing to score, and Barrington making just 5. Despite this heavy defeat to the eventual winners of the knockout competition, there was much for Stewart to smile about in 1964, especially the emergence of several promising youngsters, most notably Roger Harman, the bespectacled spin bowler, who had been patiently waiting in the wings for several years. Following Tony Lock's departure, Harman got an extended run in the side in 1964, and he proceeded to take every opportunity that came his way, finishing the summer with 129 wickets, almost twice as many as anyone else in Surrey's ranks. Harman's virtues were a high action, supported by clever flight and considerable powers of spin, and at Trent Bridge in May, Harman was almost unplayable. His efforts completely transformed the game after Surrey had trailed by 68 on first innings. Nottinghamshire had extended their lead past 130 when Harman came on. In the space of 17.1 overs, he took 8/12 as the home team were dismissed for 95, and then a fine 93 from John Edrich saw Surrey home by six wickets. In June, Harman took 8/32 at The Oval as Kent were beaten by 134 runs, and by the end of the summer, many people were predicting a bright future for the twenty-two year old from

Right: Mickey Stewart flicks a ball off his legs.

Below: Roger Harman in the Surrey squad of 1964. From left to right, standing: A. Long, R. Harman, G.G. Arnold, R.A.E. Tindall, S.J. Storey, M.D. Willett, W.A. Smith, D.A.D. Sydenham. Sitting: K.F. Barrington, M.J. Stewart, J.H. Edrich, D. Gibson.

Opposite page, left: Brian Close.

Opposite page, right: Three great Yorkshire cricketers – Geoff Boycott, Ray Illingworth and Tony Nicholson.

Hersham, who was accurate enough for Stewart to place a tight ring of close fielders around the batsmen. It looked as if he might assume Lock's mantle, but his meteoric rise was then followed by a rapid fall. In the subsequent summers, Harman began to desperately worry about failing, and after losing his line, guile, and flight, he left the Surrey staff at the end of the 1968 season.

For Yorkshire – the winners of the Championship in the previous two seasons – the summer of '64 proved to be somewhat disappointing. The side, under Brian Close's captaincy, were still able to win eleven Championship games, but even so, there were several occasions when the supremacy they had enjoyed over opponents in 1962 and 1963 was absent. Between mid-May and the middle of June, Close's team failed to win seven consecutive matches. While the inclement weather could be blamed for some of the draws, the shrewd observers of Yorkshire cricket felt the real reason was that the county's much-vaunted bowling attack had not been as effective as in previous years. Fred Trueman still produced some hostile spells at times, but there were other occasions when he failed to make the all-important early break-through with the new ball, and there was a feeling that the Yorkshire pace attack did not strike the same fear in the hearts of batsmen as in previous summers. The run of draws finally ended on 23 June at Headingley as Glamorgan were beaten by an innings and 39 runs. The comprehensive victory was largely the result of a career-best bowling performance by Tony Nicholson – the twenty-five year old from Dewsbury returned match figures of 12/73, and the young seamer went on to enjoy a fine summer. Despite an injury late in the season, Nicholson finished the summer

with a haul of 70 wickets, each coming at a shade under 14 apiece. As well as finishing on top of Yorkshire's bowling averages in Championship matches, Nicholson was rewarded with a place in the MCC tour party to South Africa. However, his back problem did not clear up in time, and Nicholson regrettably had to withdraw from the tour.

Middlesex, led in 1964 for the final time by Colin Dryborough, finished in sixth place in the Championship – exactly the same spot they had finished in the previous summer. The bowling of the Middlesex captain hit the headlines in mid-August, as the left-arm spinner took 7/94 at Northampton, including the wickets of Scott, Crump, Larter and Bailey in the space of 5 balls, with the first 3 falling in successive deliveries. Despite Dryborough's hat-trick, Middlesex lost the game by ten wickets, and Dryborough will largely be remembered for this feat, rather than being able to lift a team brimful of individual talent to the top of the county table. Nevertheless, in common with some of the other counties on Worcestershire's coat-tails, Middlesex ended the 1964 summer very well, with their final 3 home games seeing Dryborough's side inflict an innings defeat on Lancashire, before beating Northamptonshire by 145 runs and then Derbyshire by 86 runs. All three games saw Fred Titmus in fine form, with the off spinner taking 9/57 in Lancashire's second innings on a dry and dusty Lord's wicket. He followed this up with six wickets against Northants and then eleven in the match with Derbyshire. His performance in the latter game saw Titmus take his Championship tally past 100, and the summer of 1964 ended with more good news as it was confirmed that Titmus would be stepping up to the captaincy of Middlesex for 1965 following Dryborough's decision to retire from the county game. Eric Russell also enjoyed a hugely successful summer. The right-hander scored over 2,000

Colin Dryborough.   Eric Russell.

Championship runs, with centuries against Hampshire, Lancashire, Northants, Nottinghamshire and Gloucestershire. In the second half of the summer, when Mike Brearley was down from Cambridge, Middlesex boasted one of the most productive opening pairings on the county circuit, and had some of the county's seam bowlers been more on song, Middlesex might have moved up even higher in the county table.

1964 saw Kent enjoy their most successful season since 1947. For much of the season they were in the top four of the table, and had their captain, Colin Cowdrey, been free of injury for the entire season, they might have mounted a serious bid for the county title. Despite only playing in seventeen matches, Cowdrey still managed to top the county's batting averages with 1,330 runs at an average in the mid-fifties. He struck four of the fifteen Championship hundreds registered by Kent's batsmen in 1964. After being omitted from the England side, he enjoyed a real purple patch in mid-season with innings of 83 and 109 against Lancashire at Gillingham, 99 and 100* against Hampshire at Canterbury, and then 101 and 42 against Middlesex in the second match of the Canterbury Festival. On the bowling front, Alan Dixon was the county's leading wicket-taker, taking 121 Championship victims at 22 apiece. It was the first time in his career that the thirty-year-old all-rounder had passed the 100 mark, and he more than filled the vacancy left by injuries to Dave Halfyard and Alan Brown. In all, Dixon bowled over 1,000 overs, mixing his off-breaks with his medium-pace bowling with the new ball. Both are very different styles, yet it was great credit to Dixon that he could easily alternate from one to the other, without any significant loss of line or length.

Much had been expected from Somerset in 1964. They had finished up in third place in the Championship in 1963, and with largely the same players at his disposal, many

Colin Cowdrey.

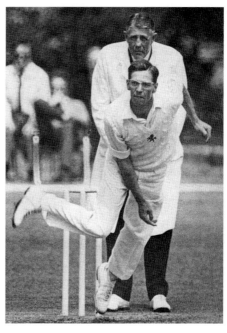

Alan Dixon.

Left: Bill Alley.

Opposite page, left: John Snow.

Opposite page, right: 'Lord Ted' Dexter.

thought that Harold Stephenson's team would mount a serious challenge for the county title. These dreams had largely evaporated inside the first month of the season, and by the middle of June, Somerset only had one Championship victory to their credit – a two-day win over Gloucestershire where off-spinner Brian Langford had exploited a dry Bath wicket to record match figures of 10/78. July saw an upswing in the county's fortunes, with well-earned victories over Essex, Worcestershire, Leicestershire and Sussex. Then in August, Fred Rumsey, the county's wholehearted left-arm quick bowler became the first Somerset man to play in Test cricket for England for sixteen years, winning selection in England's line-up for the Fourth Test against Australia at Old Trafford. By this time, Bill Alley, the forthright and brash Australian batsman, had taken over as Somerset's captain following a leg injury to the affable Harold Stephenson. After all of the pre-season hype, Stephenson had been really looking forward to the 1964 season, but it turned out to be a huge disappointment, and right from the start of the season, the wicketkeeper was bothered by the injury that, before the summer was over, had resulted in 'Steve' announcing his retirement from the county game. It was a sad end to the career of a very popular man who only twelve months before had seemed poised to astutely lead Somerset to their first county title.

Whilst 1964 saw Sussex retain the Gillette Cup, it was very different however for Ted Dexter's side in Championship cricket, where despite the rise of John Snow, their hostile new-ball bowler, the county slipped from fourth spot in 1963 down to ninth. Inconsistent and erratic, Sussex only recorded eight Championship victories during the summer. A further nine games were lost, while another ten were drawn, and throughout the summer, Sussex only passed 300 on three occasions. This lack of runs on a regular basis was one of the reasons behind the county's lack of success in the longer form of the game, and had it not been for Ian Thomson's 109 Championship wickets, Sussex might have slipped even further down the table. 1964 was John Snow's first full season of county cricket, and his haul of 72 wickets resulted in the young pace bowler winning his county cap. But as Snow later confessed in his auto-biography *Cricket Rebel*, it was often his hostility rather than any finesse that resulted in him securing this sizeable haul of scalps. The young bowler did not take kindly to any criticism, and on several occasions, anger got the better of him. A case in point was Sussex's match against Northants at Hastings, and even though he finished up on the winning side, it took some prompting from Dexter before Snow realised that the damp wicket called for the ball to be pitched up rather than being dug in short. As Snow wrote 'I was still obsessed with pace in those 1964 days and when Northants batted I dug one in a little short against Colin Milburn and it rose nicely for him to hook over square leg for four, causing our short legs to duck for cover.

'Ted was one of them and his anger was immediate – "Why don't you pitch it up, you silly little bugger?" he shouted down the wicket. Dexter or not, I didn't take too kindly to criticism like that. The next ball was about the same length. Colin went for a repeat stroke, but this ball rose a little higher than he expected, caught the shoulder of the bat, and Ted took a simple catch. "Pitch it up like that do you mean?" I shout-ed down the wicket.' With his feathers ruffled, Snow added a further five wickets to finish with 6/39 as Northants were bustled out for 85, and it was a position from which they never recovered as Sussex won by 28 runs.

Essex, under Trevor Bailey's captaincy only won eight Championship matches during 1964, and the undoubted highlight of the season was their six-wicket victory at

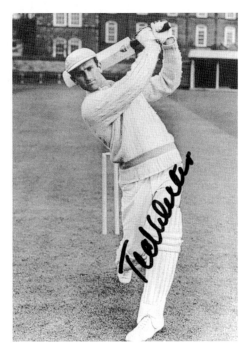

Southend over the Australians in the penultimate three-day match of their tour against county opposition. This was Essex's first win over an Australian side since 1905, and they were indebted to centuries from Gordon Barker and Keith Fletcher in building a formidable first-innings total of 425 for 6 during the first day. Trevor Bailey declared first thing on Monday morning, and he could hardly suppress his glee as the Aussies then struggled against the off-breaks of Paddy Phelan, as well as the lively seam of Ken Preston. Phelan had hitherto enjoyed a quite good season in Championship cricket, and buoyed by this success he took 5/94 as Bailey invited the Australians to follow-on – the only time on the tour that they had been put in this position. Knowing that the Southchurch Park wicket was likely to crumble, Bailey sensed a chance to defeat the tourists, and it was not long before Phelan, supported by the leg breaks of Robin Hobbs, had started to work his way through Australia's top order. Not surprisingly, there was stiffer resistance a second time around, but despite half centuries from Bill Lawry, Norman O'Neill and Brian Booth, the tourists were dismissed for 313 with Phelan adding a further five wickets to take his match haul to 10/248. Essex's target was 107 and thanks to some steady batting from Brian Taylor and Mike Bear, they reached the target for the loss of just four wickets, much to the delight of a large crowd of Essex enthusiasts, supplemented by many holidaymakers who had visited the Thames-side resort.

Glamorgan were another county to defeat the Australians during their 1964 tour with the Welsh county's victory coming at the start of August in front of a jubilant

Trevor Bailey.   Paddy Phelan.

crowd at the St Helen's ground in Swansea. The stars of this Welsh win were off-cutter Don Shepherd, who recorded match figures of 9/93, and Jim Pressdee, whose accurate left-arm spin resulted in a match haul of 10/123. 1964 was a wonderful summer for Presdee, who in the early part of his career had, at times, seemed almost reluctant to bowl and had become largely a batsman who only bowled occasionally. Things changed in the 1960s, and in 1964 Pressdee completed the Double of 1,000 runs and 100 wickets for the second successive summer – a wonderful way to celebrate his Benefit season. The thirty-one year old from the Mumbles only hit one century – an unbeaten 133 against Essex at Clacton, but his consistent run-scoring in Glamorgan's middle order saw him past the 1,000 mark. On the bowling front, his best Championship performance came at the Arms Park in mid-July where he took 8/78 in Lancashire's first innings, including a spell of 6/14 in 8 overs. The victory over the Australians, and Pressdee's all-round feats were the highlight of a quite modest season for Glamorgan. They began and ended the summer with Championship wins, but in between there was little for Glamorgan supporters to get excited about, with Ossie Wheatley's side winning a mere 7 Championship matches. The washout of seven entire days did not help matters, and several of the Welsh club's young prospects failed to make the headway that many had expected. Don Shepherd, who the previous summer had claimed 126 wickets, finished with just 78 Championship victims. But at least he had the satisfaction of passing Jack Mercer's club record of 1,641 wickets, and for the first time in his career 'Shep' recorded a hat-trick, dismissing three Northants' batsmen in succession in the

Ossie Wheatley bowling for Glamorgan against Essex in 1969.

Left: Jim Pressdee.

Opposite page, left: Colin Ingleby-Mackenzie.

Opposite page, right: Derek Shackleton – in bowling action.

visitors' second innings of their match at Swansea, which ended in a comfortable seven-wicket win for the Welsh county.

Derbyshire had ended the 1963 season at the bottom of the Championship table, and for the first part of 1964, it seemed as if the Peakites would occupy seventeenth spot again. On 23 June, they eventually won their first Championship game of the summer, and it was to the credit of Charlie Lee's team that they won a further four games and rose up to twelfth place in the competition, with twice as many points as in the previous disastrous season. In their match against the Australians in mid-June, Derbyshire gave a tangible sign that headway was being made. After Laurie Johnson, had struck a century in Derbyshire's first innings – the first ever for the county against the Australians – Lee played a fine captain's innings when his side batted again. Lee struck a dozen boundaries in a bold display of strokeplay, and was unbeaten on 80 when he eschewed thoughts of personal glory and a century against the tourists by declaring and setting the Australians a target of 250 in a fraction under three hours. Wickets then fell at regular intervals, especially against Edwin Smith's off spin, and never at any stage of their innings did the tourists look like reaching the target. There were times in the final half-hour of the game when it looked as if Derbyshire might record a fairytale victory, but the Australians' ninth-wicket pair held out for the draw. While Lee was pleased at the county's improved form, 1964 ended on a rather disap-pointing note for the Derbyshire captain. He increasingly suffered from cartilage trouble, and the persistent injury caused him initially to miss several games in the final few weeks, and then at the end of summer, it prompted him into announcing his retirement from the county game.

Although Hampshire defeated both Worcestershire, the champions, and Warwickshire, the runners-up, 1964 was a largely disappointing season for the South Coast club. As *Wisden's* correspondent noted, 'had Hampshire shown the same application and determination during the rest of the season as they did in those two matches, they might have finished on a more propitious note. As it was, half their matches were drawn, many of them after Hampshire failed to press home an initial advantage.' There were other times when lady luck did not smile on Colin Ingleby-Mackenzie, the dashing Hampshire captain, and twice during the season Roy Marshall, the prolific opening batsman, broke fingers, and then in August he fractured a toe and spent another spell on the sidelines. On the bowling front, Ingleby-Mackenzie relied largely on his new-ball pairing of Derek Shackleton and 'Butch' White. For many years, Shackleton had been the 'Mr Reliable' of the Hampshire attack, and for twenty consecutive seasons, the steady seam bowler took over 100 wickets. In 1964 he became the first bowler in the country to reach the century mark, achieving the feat just days before his fortieth birthday. The lion-hearted seamer finished the summer with 138 Championship wickets to his name – a worthy reward after once again shouldering the burden of the attack, and bowling 1,370 overs.

1964 was Lancashire's Centenary Year, but any thoughts of glorious celebrations were erased by a dismal playing record, as Ken Grieves' team recorded just four victories in their twenty-eight games. The Old Trafford club was also racked by internal trouble and strife, which culminated in several players being released, a change of captain and secretary, plus a special meeting of members, when by an overwhelming margin, feelings of dissatisfaction were expressed at the running of the cricket affairs.

The club had to wait until 3 July before recording their first Championship victory, and the only ray of sunshine in what became a very difficult summer, both on and off the field, was the consistent form shown by Brian Statham. The sterling seamer went on to take over 100 Championship wickets, but the deficiencies in Lancashire's

Left: Brian Statham.

Opposite: Carlton Forbes and the rest of the Nottinghamshire side walking out from the pavilion at Rodney Parade, Newport.

batting and bowling were exposed at the end of August when the county were beaten in their Centenary Celebration Match by the MCC. Just to rub salt into the Mancunian wounds, the defeat was initiated by some fine bowling in Lancashire's second innings by two Yorkshiremen – Fred Trueman and Don Wilson, while in the MCC's first innings, two of the great names from the county's past, Jack Ikin aged forty-six, and Cyril Washbrook, aged forty-nine, had shared an opening stand of 139. The Centenary Match also coincided with the leaking to the press of the findings of an internal review, undertaken by team manager Cyril Washbrook, following concerns about the loss of form, and the poor behaviour of some players. Among the bombshells leaked to the press were details of the committee's decision to release Peter Marner, Geoff Clayton, Jack Dyson and captain Ken Grieves, who had not exactly seen eye to eye with Washbrook. It all became a sorry mess, and the club had to hastily issue a statement, in which they 'regretted the publicity given to the question of the captaincy before they had an opportunity to interview Grieves'. The statement went on to add that the club aimed 'to build up a new team, who can be relied upon to conduct themselves well and pay a proper respect to the captain at all times'. How the Lancashire supporters must have enjoyed their New Year celebrations and to finally bid farewell to a sad and unhappy chapter in the history of the famous club.

Nottinghamshire were delighted to welcome HRH The Duke of Edinburgh to Trent Bridge on the opening day of the First Test against Australia. The Duke arrived by helicopter, but sadly the weather intervened, and rain prevented him from seeing any play. The Duke's visit rather epitomised what became something of a damp squib for Nottinghamshire in 1964, as the county side, led by wicketkeeper Geoff Millman,

finished in fifteenth place in the county table and recorded a mere four Championship wins. An innings victory over Leicestershire in the opening game of the summer raised hopes, but the next victory did not come until the first week of July, and when the final analysis was made of the 1964 season, perhaps the most telling statistic for Nottinghamshire was that their four victories – over Gloucestershire (twice), Leicestershire and Lancashire – were all against the counties in the bottom-four places of the table. The man who headed Nottinghamshire's bowling averages for 1964 was West Indian fast bowler Carlton Forbes. The Jamaican claimed 53 Championship wickets at a fraction under 18 runs apiece, and he was one of the new breed of county players in the 1960s, as forward-thinking counties such as Nottinghamshire hired an increasing number of players, especially from the Caribbean. Forbes had first come to the club's attention playing for Middlesbrough in the Yorkshire League. Although he had made his county debut in 1959, the summer of 1964 proved to be a turning point in his career. It was the third time he had passed the fifty mark for the season, but never before had his wickets come so cheaply. 1964 was therefore something of a turning point in the West Indian's career as in each of the following three summers, Forbes took over 100 wickets, and by the time he retired in 1973, he had 707 first-class wickets to his name.

1964 was also a depressing season for Leicestershire, and like their neighbours at Trent Bridge, the East Midlands county endured a long barren spell when defeats almost became commonplace, as Maurice Hallam's side lost 11 games in succession. In the end they lost 18 matches – more than in any season since 1945. Only three matches were won, and in each case, Leicestershire just managed to scrape home

Maurice Hallam.   Terry Spencer.

before stumps were drawn. Gloucestershire were defeated at Grace Road with the penultimate ball of the match. There were only five minutes remaining at Portsmouth when Hampshire were beaten by five wickets, and a successful run-chase was mounted against Glamorgan at Grace Road with Clive Inman and Brian Booth steering the county home with only a quarter of an hour remaining. The cares of captaincy appeared to weigh on the mind of Maurice Hallam. The gifted strokemaker missed several games through illness and injury, and he failed to pass 1,000 runs for the season for the first time since 1954. Three others though did achieve the feat for the Leicester club – Booth, Inman and Stanley Jayasinghe, the Ceylonese right-hander. On the bowling front, Terry Spencer was the club's most successful bowler, and for the first time in the 1950s and 1960s, Leicestershire were glad to be able to lean heavily on the wholehearted seam bowler. Spencer had first played for the county back in 1952, having come to the attention of the county in a pre-season friendly when the twenty year old clean bowled the captain Charles Palmer and sent his off stump cartwheeling out of the ground. Spencer proceeded to play in every one of Leicestershire's Championship games in 1952, and after completing his National Service, he became a mainstay of the county's attack. 1961 was Spencer's most successful season, as he claimed 123 wickets at 19 runs apiece – a performance that saw him included on the selectors' short list for the MCC winter tour to India.

Gloucestershire propped up the Championship table, with just three victories to their credit. It was something of a marked decline for Ken Graveney's team, as the West Country side had finished in fourth spot in 1962 and then eighth in 1963. The latter had been Graveney's first year in charge after a dramatic return to the county game for a man who had initially played the county in the late 1940s as a fast-medium out-swing bowler. Back ailments had forced Graveney into retirement from the county game in 1951, but as his disc problems eased, he returned to the county's

Second XI in the late 1950s, before leading them with much success in 1962. A few eyebrows were raised when the committee offered Graveney the captaincy of the First XI in 1963, but the thirty-nine year old soon silenced the doubters, and he proved himself to be a most capable leader as the county maintained their place in the top half of the county table. They might have remained there in 1964 had it not been for the lack of a genuine fast bowler, as well as the absence for much of the season through injury of Arthur Milton, their reliable top-order batsman. Milton sustained a badly fractured right arm in the county's opening match of the season against Oxford University at The Parks. At the time of the injury, Milton was unbeaten on 83, and seemed well on course to register the club's first hundred of the 1964 campaign. But he was then hit on the arm while standing as the non-striker, as his batting partner John Mortimore attempted a fierce drive against the student bowlers. After this freak injury, Milton was out of action until mid-July, and in Gloucestershire's match against Derbyshire at Lydney he showed what the county had been missing by repeatedly cutting and pulling the visiting bowlers in making 70 and 68★. But after appearing in half a dozen matches, Milton was then injured again, and he missed the final six games of the summer.

Leading First-Class Batting Averages for 1964

(Qualification: minimum of 10 innings)

Name	Matches	Inns	NO	Runs	HS	Ave	100	50
K.F. Barrington	22	35	5	1,872	256	62.40	4	9
R.B. Simpson	22	38	8	1,714	311	57.13	5	10
B.C. Booth	23	36	8	1,551	193★	55.39	3	10
M.C. Cowdrey	23	37	5	1,763	117	55.09	4	12
T.W. Graveney	30	51	7	2,385	164	54.20	5	16
G. Boycott	27	44	4	2,110	177	52.75	6	11
R.M. Cowper	20	29	4	1,286	113	51.44	3	9
M.J. Stewart	24	44	5	1,980	227★	50.76	6	6
R.C. Wilson	28	49	5	2,038	156	46.31	4	14
W.E. Russell	31	56	5	2,342	193	45.92	5	15
M.D. Willett	29	51	12	1,789	126	45.87	4	10
N.C. O'Neill	20	34	4	1,369	151	45.63	4	7
J.M. Brearley	29	54	5	2,179	169	44.46	5	11
E.R. Dexter	27	49	5	1,948	174	44.27	5	9
W.M. Lawry	24	41	3	1,601	121	42.13	5	10
G. Pullar	29	53	5	1,974	132★	41.12	3	15
J.H. Edrich	26	45	3	1,727	124	41.11	2	12
S.E. Leary	22	37	7	1,190	137★	39.66	1	8
M.J. Smith	20	30	11	743	108★	39.10	1	3
M.J.K. Smith	30	50	6	1,691	132	38.43	1	13
K. Taylor	21	33	2	1,173	160	37.83	2	6

J.S. Pressdee	32	54	11	1,606	133★	37.34	1	11
R. Illingworth	33	44	9	1,301	135	37.17	2	7
P.J.P. Burge	23	34	4	1,114	160	37.13	2	6
P.H. Parfitt	23	38	3	1,290	200★	36.85	5	2
D.C. Morgan	30	50	6	1,616	147	36.72	3	8
J.W.T. Wilcox	10	14	4	367	63	36.70	0	3
J.M. Parks	28	48	7	1,481	103★	36.12	1	13
D.A. Livingstone	30	53	6	1,671	124	35.55	4	7
R.G.A. Headley	31	53	5	1,697	117★	35.35	4	9
R.M. Prideaux	32	55	1	1,867	153	34.57	2	13
T.R. Veivers	22	28	7	725	79	34.52	0	7

Batsmen Scoring Over 1,500 Runs in First-Class Cricket in 1964

Name	Matches	Inns	NO	Runs	100	50
T.W. Graveney	30	51	7	2,385	5	16
W.E. Russell	31	56	5	2,342	5	15
J.M. Brearley	29	54	5	2,179	5	11
G. Boycott	27	44	4	2,110	6	11
R.C. Wilson	28	49	5	2,038	4	14
M.J. Stewart	24	44	5	1,980	6	6
G. Pullar	29	53	5	1,974	3	15
J.B. Bolus	34	66	7	1,961	3	14
E.R. Dexter	27	49	5	1,948	5	9
R.B. Nicholls	32	61	1	1,912	2	14
K.F. Barrington	22	35	5	1,872	4	9
R.M. Prideaux	32	55	1	1,867	2	13
M.J. Horton	32	57	3	1,824	3	11
M.D. Willett	29	51	12	1,789	4	10
M.C. Cowdrey	23	37	5	1,763	4	12
J.H. Edrich	26	45	3	1,727	2	12
K.G. Suttle	31	57	3	1,722	3	9
R.B. Simpson	22	38	8	1,714	5	10
G. Barker	30	57	1	1,707	3	9
R.G.A. Headley	31	53	5	1,697	4	9
M.J.K. Smith	30	50	6	1,691	1	13
D.A. Livingstone	30	53	6	1,671	4	7
K.W.R. Fletcher	34	61	9	1,616	2	9
D.C. Morgan	30	50	6	1,616	3	8
J.S. Pressdee	32	54	11	1,606	1	11
W.M. Lawry	24	41	3	1,601	5	10
D.M. Green	31	59	4	1,577	2	9
R.W. Barber	31	54	4	1,573	3	7
M.J. Bear	31	58	5	1,567	1	9

A. Jones	31	56	3	1,558	1	12
B.C. Booth	23	36	8	1,551	3	10
Khalid Ibadulla	29	51	1	1,547	4	5
B.L. Reynolds	29	51	2	1,534	2	9

Leading First-Class Bowling Averages for 1964

(Qualification: minimum fifteen wickets)

Name	Balls	Mdns	Runs	Wkts	BB	Ave	5wI	10wM
J.A. Standen	2,534	131	832	64	7–30	13.00	6	0
L.J. Coldwell	4,417	211	1,518	98	7–25	15.48	7	1
A.G. Nicolson	3,490	159	1,193	76	7–32	15.69	6	1
T.W. Cartwright	6,878	501	2,141	134	7–28	15.97	8	1
R.R. Bailey	763	34	273	17	5–25	16.05	3	0
N.I. Thomson	5,543	293	1,891	116	10–49	16.30	6	1
F.J. Titmus	6,873	441	2,106	123	9–57	17.12	6	2
R. Illingworth	6,074	374	2,131	122	7–49	17.46	7	1
C. Forbes	2,655	143	950	53	7–80	17.92	2	1
J.A. Flavell	4,719	170	1,934	107	9–56	18.07	6	2
D.A.D. Sydenham	3,756	176	1,503	82	9–70	18.32	7	2
N. Gifford	5,873	399	2,123	114	7–31	18.62	5	1
T. Greenhough	1,556	68	658	35	7–56	18.79	4	1
P.J. Watts	3,105	135	1,178	62	6–28	19.00	4	0
D.J. Brown	4,204	184	1,648	86	8–64	19.16	4	2
M.E. Scott	6,226	426	2,178	113	7–32	19.27	6	2
J.S. Pressdee	4,638	204	2,036	105	8–78	19.39	7	2
J.D. Bannister	3,412	194	1,077	55	6–16	19.58	2	0
B.A. Langford	5,834	379	2,059	105	7–42	19.60	7	3
N.J.N. Hawke	4,452	211	1,644	83	6–19	19.80	6	0
D.S. Steele	1,426	91	538	27	4–15	19.92	0	0
J.B. Statham	5,260	170	2,203	110	8–37	20.02	6	1
F.E. Rumsey	4,223	158	1,617	80	7–34	20.21	3	0
K.E. Palmer	5,827	275	2,120	104	7–34	20.38	7	0
D. Shackleton	8,622	568	2,897	142	8–27	20.40	10	1
R.V. Webster	2,269	113	943	46	7–6	20.50	4	1
B.S. Crump	5,212	283	1,685	82	6–52	20.54	2	0
D. Wilson	5,798	355	2,111	102	6–51	20.69	4	1
R.G.M. Carter	2,268	95	837	40	6–45	20.92	2	1
D.J. Shepherd	5,858	395	1,822	87	5–20	20.94	4	0
R. Harman	6,787	386	2,858	136	8–12	21.01	11	2
P.I. Pocock	1,615	88	698	33	4–24	21.15	0	0
O.S. Wheatley	5,407	277	1,869	88	7–72	21.23	4	0
J.D.F. Larter	5,036	200	2,043	96	5–34	21.28	2	0

W.E. Alley	3,886	214	1,365	64	6-116	21.32	4	0
D.N.F. Slade	3,192	231	1,003	47	6-15	21.34	1	0
J.B. Mortimore	6,218	323	2,230	104	7-69	21.44	6	1

Leading Wicket-Takers in First-Class Cricket in 1964

Name	Balls	Mdns	Runs	Wkts	BB
D. Shackleton	8,622	568	2,897	142	8-27
R. Harman	6,787	386	2,858	136	8-12
T.W. Cartwright	6,878	501	2,141	134	7-28
F.J. Titmus	6,873	441	2,106	123	9-57
R. Illingworth	6,074	374	2,131	122	7-49
A.L. Dixon	6,700	310	2,915	122	8-61
N.I. Thomson	5,543	293	1,891	116	10-49
N. Gifford	5,873	399	2,123	114	7-31
M.E. Scott	6,226	426	2,178	113	7-32
J.B. Statham	5,260	170	2,203	110	8-37
J.A. Flavell	4,719	170	1,934	107	9-56
J.S. Pressdee	4,638	204	2,036	105	8-78
B.A. Langford	5,834	379	2,059	105	7-42
K.E. Palmer	5,827	275	2,120	104	7-34
J.B. Mortimore	6,218	323	2,230	104	7-69
D.W. White	6,066	185	3,149	104	6-33
D. Wilson	5,798	355	2,111	102	6-51
D.L. Underwood	6,417	432	2,450	101	9-28
F.S. Trueman	4,999	171	2,194	100	5-48
B.R. Knight	6,209	215	2,704	100	6-81
L.J. Coldwell	4,417	211	1,518	98	7-25
J.D.F. Larter	5,036	200	2,043	96	5-34
S. Ramadhin	5,713	305	2,046	92	8-121
O.S. Wheatley	5,407	277	1,869	88	7-72
G.D. McKenzie	5,029	217	1,976	88	7-153
D.J. Shepherd	5,858	395	1,822	87	5-20
D.J. Brown	4,204	184	1,648	86	8-64
A.S. Brown	5,692	220	2,392	85	5-42
N.J.N. Hawke	4,452	211	1,644	83	6-19
D.A.D. Sydenham	3,756	176	1,503	82	9-70
B.S. Crump	5,212	283	1,685	82	6-52
I.J. Davison	4,674	181	1,982	82	7-68
A.B. Jackson	5,009	190	1,979	81	5-42
R.N.S. Hobbs	4,563	148	2,342	81	6-73
F.E. Rumsey	4,223	158	1,617	80	7-34

The Leading Fielders in First-Class Cricket in 1964

Wicketkeepers

100	R. Booth	(91 ct, 9 st)
78	A. Long	(69 ct, 9 st)
77	B.S.V. Timms	(59 ct, 18 st)
76	B. Taylor	(59 ct, 10 st)
75	B.J. Meyer	(59 ct, 16 st)
74	K.V. Andrew	(67 ct, 7 st)
71	J.T. Murray	(58 ct, 13 st)
69	J.G. Binks	(57 ct, 12 st)
66	G. Millman	(56 ct, 10 st)
65	M.G. Griffith	(59 ct, 6 st)
64	R.W. Taylor	(58 ct, 6 st)
64	J.M. Parks	(53 ct, 11 st)
58	A.C. Smith	(53 ct, 5 st)
53	G. Clayton	(46 ct, 7 st)

Fielders

46	D.W. Richardson
45	R.G.A. Headley
42	C.M. Milburn
38	K.B. Ibadulla
38	P.M. Walker
37	M.J.K. Smith
36	P.D. Watts
35	R. Virgin
32	S.J. Storey
31	J.S. Pressdee

The 1964 Australians

They were hailed as the weakest Australian party ever chosen to travel to England for an Ashes series. Eight of the seventeen-man party had never played in England before, and without the recently retired Richie Benaud, Neil Harvey and Alan Davidson, the 1964 Australians certainly had an inexperienced line-up. As Denis Compton wrote, 'this was the most under-rated, the most frequently written-off Australian team I had ever known. Even before they left for England, they were being dismissed as of no account, with the return of the Ashes to England being little more than a formality.' At twenty-eight, Bobby Simpson was the youngest Australian captain to visit the UK in the twentieth century, and was chosen after leading Australia in their drawn series against South Africa. A shrewd and knowledgeable leader, he was criticised in the Springbok series for attempting too much – opening the batting, fielding at slip and leading the side. His parents hailed from the Falkirk area of Scotland and emigrated to Sydney in the 1920s. Simpson's father had played professional football, but like his brothers, Bobby took to cricket and made his debut for New South Wales at the age of sixteen.

Brian Booth was the vice-captain of the tour party, yet the thirty-year-old school-master arrived in Britain without ever having led a team in a first-class match. He played his domestic cricket in Australia under Simpson's leadership, and was renowned as a graceful strokemaker, caressing the ball rather than clubbing it to the boundary, and in his eleven Tests prior to the '64 series, he had already passed fifty on nine occasions.

On the previous tour in 1961, Bill Lawry had enjoyed a highly successful summer, amassing over 2,000 runs, and striking centuries in the Tests at Lord's and Old Trafford. By the time he arrived in England, the left-hander was regarded as the most difficult opener in Test cricket to dislodge, and the Australians were hoping for another highly productive summer from the Victorian.

Ian Redpath was the third and least experienced opening batsman in the party. However, there was no doubting the flair and application that the twenty-three year old showed for Victoria, and in the tour party's farewell match in Western Australia, he had made an impressive double century. If Simpson was going to drop down the order, Redpath was likely to move up to open the innings with Lawry, his state partner, but before arriving in England, Redpath only had a single Test cap to his name.

Norm O'Neill had a fine record in 32 Tests for Australia, and in 1961, he had enjoyed a highly productive tour, finishing only 19 runs short of 2,000. But in the months leading up to the tour, O'Neill had been suffering from knee problems, and his lack of fitness meant that he did not score a century in domestic matches until the farewell game for the touring party in Perth.

The 1964 Australians – from left to right, back row: Arthur James (masseur), Neil Hawke, Graham Corling, Johnny Martin, Bob Cowper, Alan Connelly, David Sherwood (scorer). Middle row: Rex Sellers, Tom Veivers, Jack Potter, Jack Ledward (asst manager), Graham McKenzie, Ian Redpath, Barry Jarman. Front row: Peter Burge, Norman O'Neill, Bobby Simpson (captain), Ray Steele (manager), Brian Booth, Bill Lawry, Wally Grout.

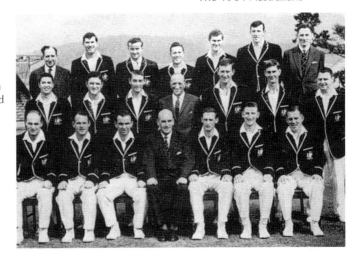

Bobby Simpson square cuts David Allan at the Sydney Cricket Ground in November 1962.

Brian Booth.

Clockwise from top left:

Bill Lawry.

Norman O'Neill batting.

Norman O'Neill smiling!

Opposite page, left: Bob Cowper.

Opposite page, right: Jack Potter.

Peter Burge was making his third tour of England, and the thirty-one year old had 29 Tests to his name. But some critics considered the solidly built Queenslander to be very fortunate to be chosen for the 1964 tour as he was starting to slow down in the field, and in the eyes of his detractors, some of the younger and more mobile batsmen deserved a chance ahead of him.

Bob Cowper and Jack Potter were two of the emerging young batsmen in Shield cricket. Cowper had played some impressive innings for Victoria, and the twenty-three year old had probably clinched a place in the party with unbeaten scores of 104 and 88 against the clock in the Sheffield Shield match against Queensland at Brisbane. However, he was untried at Test level. The same could be said about Jack Potter, the twenty-six-year-old Victorian, who had been a consistent and assertive batsman in State cricket, as well as being a fine fielder.

Wally Grout was the senior member of the tour party. The thirty-seven year old was one of the finest wicketkeepers in the world, and his homespun, earthy wit had made him one of Test cricket's most engaging and popular characters. He had spent ten years waiting in the wings as understudy to Don Tallon, and had subsequently established many wicketkeeping records, especially with the number of catches off Alan Davidson. But 'Davo' had now gone into retirement, and some were wondering how much longer Wally would continue.

Barry Jarman had been Grout's understudy behind the stumps for the past seven years. In the 1962/63 series he had deputised for Grout in four Tests, and there was speculation that the South Australian would get greater opportunities on the Ashes tour.

Graham McKenzie was highly regarded as a Test bowler, with the twenty-two year old from Western Australia being regarding as having the ability to turn a match in the space of an over, as well as having the strength and stamina to survive the most arduous day in the field. He had bowled well in tandem with Alan Davidson, but in the

recent series with South Africa, he had missed his sparring partner and had taken time to adjust to the new front-foot law for no balls.

Neil Hawke had made his Test debut in the Fifth Test of the 1962/63 series, and the twenty-five year old was considered to be a key member of the tour party, especially as many felt that his brisk swerve and seam bowling would be invaluable in English conditions. But in his 5 Tests before the Ashes tour, Hawke's 16 wickets had cost 35 runs apiece.

Alan Connelly had made his Test debut in the preceding series against the Springboks. Regarded as one of fastest bowlers in Australia, he was starting to expand his repertoire so that he did not just rely on sheer pace, and the tall and loose-limbed Victorian had tried to cut the ball off the pitch, as well as experimenting with a slower 'knuckle' ball, with his forefingers doubled up behind the ball.

Tom Veivers had yet to really establish himself as a Test-class bowler. The twenty-seven year old was a forthright left-handed batsman, but his off spin had been harshly dealt with by England's batsmen in two matches in the 1962/63 rubber. He had returned in the series against South Africa to bowl with greater accuracy and economy, but he still lacked penetration at international level.

Johnny Martin had experience of English conditions having played in the Lancashire Leagues, but he was making his first major tour. At thirty-three, he was the second-oldest member of the tour party, although his all-round skills were likely to come in handy, with left-arm spin delivered out of the back of his hand, coupled with forceful strokeplay and safe fielding up close or in the deep.

Rex Sellers was another uncapped bowler, and the leg-spinner owed his selection to a wonderful season with South Australia that helped them win the Sheffield Shield.

Opposite: Bobby Simpson (centre) and Barry Jarman (right) in jolly mood.

Right: Graham McKenzie.

Even so, he still had only 82 first-class wickets to his name. But these were riches compared with Grahame Corling, the least-known and youngest face in the Australian party. He was also considered to be something of a gamble, with only 25 first-class wickets to his name. His bowling for the New South Wales Country XI had impressed the MCC batsmen on their tour Down Under in 1962/63, and some consistent performances for the State side led to the selectors opting for the raw twenty-three year old.

Despite the presence of many inexperienced players in the Australian party, the tourists proved their doubters wrong and returned home having won the series and retained the Ashes. The success owed much to the captaincy and batting of Bobby Simpson, the strokeplay of Peter Burge, and the fiery bowling of Graham McKenzie, who took 29 wickets in the five-match Test series to equal the record set by Clarrie Grimmett for the most wickets by an Australian in Tests in England. As the tour progressed, other Australian bowlers steadily grew in confidence, and just to compound things, the much-vaunted English attack rather went off the boil. Rather than finding wickets easy pickings, they became meat and drink to the increasingly impressive Australian batsmen. Back in May, the question had been who was going to take wickets for Australia, but by August it was now a case of who was going to dismiss their batsmen?

None of this looked at all likely in the opening weeks of the tour as the novices tried to adjust to English conditions, and were also hit by a combination of rain and injury scares. Their early preparations at Lord's were hampered by wet and murky weather, while Sellers developed a cyst on the third finger of his bowling hand, and missed the opening few weeks of the tour in order to have medical treatment in

London. Simpson also required hospital treatment after sustaining a neck injury, while Hawke needed check-ups on his left knee. For much of the opening week of the tour, the tourists had to make do with indoor nets at Finchley, and there was much relief in the Australian camp when they won their opening tour game, defeating the Duke of Norfolk's XI by four wickets in their one-day contest at Arundel. O'Neill top-scored with an assured 61, while Corling was the leading bowler with 3/22; a feat made even more impressive given the fact that the youngster had left his bowling boots in his London hotel room. Les Lenham, the twelfth man for the Duke's team lent Corling his boots, and the Australian responded with the wickets of Roy Marshall, the Rev. David Sheppard and Ted Dexter – not bad for starters!

As the tourists made their way to Worcester for the traditional curtain-raiser to their matches against the counties, the newspapers were full of previews about the Australians, with the English journalists weighing up the strengths and weaknesses of Simpson's party. Many were quick to write off the tourists, and the noises coming out of the Australian camp apparently showed that Simpson himself was not brimming with confidence. At a press conference early in the tour, he was asked by Brian Johnston of the BBC by what margin he would like to win the series. Simpson's laconic reply was 'I'll be quite happy to go one up in the last Test!' There were other occasions as well when Simpson appeared not at all confident about his bowling resources. In the game with Somerset at Taunton, and then again at Cardiff in the match against Glamorgan, Simpson erred on the side of caution when setting the counties a target. In both games, he opted to bat on when perhaps he might have declared, and even in the match against Cambridge University, the tourists struggled to dismiss the students.

The first sign of an upswing in morale in the tourist's camp came in the week before the First Test when they defeated an MCC side containing many players who were pressing for Test honours. Corling and McKenzie impressed with the ball, as few of the aspiring England players got on top of the Australian attack. O'Neill and Simpson then dominated the MCC attack, with both batsmen making impressive and assured centuries against the left-arm pace of David Sydenham, and the right-arm quicks of John Price. Both were highly regarded on the county circuit, but neither could contain the tourists, and the outcome was a comprehensive nine-wicket win for the Australians.

The mood in the English media also began to change and soon after their victory over the MCC, a few of the national writers began tipping Australia to win the Test series. E.M. Wellings was one of the respected journalists who was convinced that the tourists would have the upper hand – 'from events at the season start, the Test match odds must have shifted in favour of Australia. Based on what English players have not yet done and what the Australians have achieved, I would put the odds at six to four… The greatest single factor against England is the current indifferent form of Trueman on whom rested our main bowling hopes before the season started. He appears to be carrying too much weight for a pace bowler.'

There was therefore a growing confidence in Australian ranks as they headed to Nottingham in early June for the opening Test of the Ashes series. The young bowlers had started to acclimatise, and the batsmen had some decent scores under their belts. With the exception of Sellers, the tourists were fit and raring to go, but the same could not be said about all of the England XI, who were rocked by injury to John Edrich. The left-handed opener from Surrey had jarred an ankle the day before the start of

Fred Titmus batting for Middlesex against Kent.

the First Test, after treading on the ball in the Trent Bridge nets. By the end of the prac-
tice session, he was free of pain, and no replacements were sought. However, the following morning, Edrich was in a lot of discomfort, and after having a net with
Coldwall, Edrich withdrew from the side barely an hour before the start of the series.
The net effect was that Titmus was promoted up the order from number eight as a
makeshift opener with Boycott, and after a delayed start, Dexter won the toss, and this
untried and unexpected combination of Boycott and Titmus started the series that
everyone had been eagerly anticipating.

It nearly began in very dramatic fashion with Boycott's first ball in Test cricket
almost being his last as McKenzie bowled a perfect away-swinger. The first delivery of
the match pitched off stump and moved away sharply as Boycott played and missed
the ball by a hair's breadth. The Yorkshireman soon settled in, although the visiting
attack extracted some alarming lift off the surface, while there was lavish lateral movement. With the score on 38, Hawke removed Titmus, but after eighty-five minutes the
rain clouds returned, and Boycott and Dexter must have been relieved to return to the
pavilion with their wickets intact.

After the rain the previous day, play began on the second morning in overcast conditions that were a seam bowler's paradise – something that the English attack would
surely have utilised, but on this occasion, the Australian bowlers did not fully exploit
the damp surface. However, wickets still fell as England's batsmen went on the attack
and perished in the cause. Barrington lofted a ball straight to Lawry at wide long on,

and later Parks, after taking 12 off an over from Veivers, pulled him into the hands of Booth at square leg.

Rain washed out play on Saturday, and for the rest of the weekend there was a lot of speculation about how the Australians would fare when it came to their turn to bat on Monday. As expected the seamers extracted movement, while the spinners got some turn, but the surface was not as spiteful as on Friday. There was no more menacing lift or extravagant movement, but none of the Australian batsmen really got on top of the workmanlike English attack. The home team gained a 48-run lead on first innings, and after the close there was a lot of talk about what might have happened had the tourists batted earlier in the match. With so much time lost to rain, Dexter realised that his team's best hope of a victory was to go for quick runs, so with Boycott nursing a cracked finger, the England captain promoted himself to open, taking 15 in an over from debutant Corling shortly before the close. Dexter continued in positive mode the following morning, but on 68 he fell to a fine diving catch by O'Neill. Barrington and Cowdrey found it difficult to maintain the momentum, and it was Jim Parks who upped the tempo, allowing Dexter to declare shortly after lunch on the final day, leaving Australia a target of 242 in 193 minutes.

Dexter was immediately rewarded with the wicket of Lawry in the opening over, as he attempted to take two runs to Coldwell at midwicket. In then walked O'Neill who began a battle royal with Trueman. Four successive bouncers from 'Fiery Fred' were all hooked to the boundary, but at the other end, Redpath was caught behind off Flavell by a ball that cut away. Flavell then twice hit O'Neill on his right hand, forcing the Australian to retire with severe bruising and swelling, but just as England appeared to be on top, the rain returned and washed out the rest of the match.

Bobby Simpson introduces the Australian team to HRH The Queen Mother during the tourists' match at Arundel.

England *v.* Australia (First Test)
Trent Bridge, Nottingham
4, 5, 6, 8, 9 June 1964

Result: Match Drawn
Toss: England
Umpires: J.S. Buller and C.S. Elliott

England First Innings					Second Innings			
G. Boycott	c Simpson	b Corling	48					
F.J. Titmus	c Redpath	b Hawke	16		lbw		b McKenzie	17
*E.R. Dexter	c Grout	b Hawke	9	(1)	c O'Neill		b McKenzie	68
M.C. Cowdrey		b Hawke	32	(3)			b McKenzie	33
K.F. Barrington	c Lawry	b Veivers	22	(4)	lbw		b Corling	33
P.J. Sharpe	not out		35	(6)			c & b Veivers	1
+J.M. Parks	c Booth	b Veivers	15	(5)	c Hawke		b Veivers	19
F.S. Trueman	c Simpson	b Veivers	0	(7)	c Grout		b McKenzie	4
D.A. Allen	c Grout	b McKenzie	21	(8)	lbw		b McKenzie	3
L.J. Coldwell	not out		0	(10)	not out			0
J.A. Flavell				(9)	c Booth		b Corling	7
Extras	(b 5, lb 11, nb 2)		18		(b 2, lb 2, w 1, nb 3)			8
Total	(8 wickets declared)		216		(9 wickets declared)			193

FoW: 1-38, 2-70, 3-90, 4-135, 5-141, 6-164, 7-165, 8-212

1-90, 2-95, 3-147, 4-174, 5-179, 6-180, 7-186, 8-187, 9-193

Bowling	O	M	R	W	O	M	R	W
McKenzie	28	7	53	1	24	5	53	5
Corling	23	7	38	1	15.5	4	54	2
Hawke	35	15	68	3	19	5	53	0
Veivers	16	2	39	3	8	0	25	2

Australia First Innings				Second Innings	
W.M. Lawry	c Barrington	b Coldwell	11	run out	3
I.R. Redpath		b Trueman	6	c Parks b Flavell	2
N.C. O'Neill		b Allen	26	retired hurt	24
P.J.P. Burge	lbw	b Trueman	31	not out	4
B.C. Booth	run out		0	not out	6
*R.B. Simpson	c Barrington	b Titmus	50		
T.R. Veivers	c Trueman	b Flavell	8		
G.D. McKenzie	c Parks	b Coldwell	4		
N.J.N. Hawke	not out		10		
+A.T.W. Grout	c Parks	b Coldwell	13		
G.E. Corling		b Trueman	3		

| Extras | (lb 1, nb 5) | | 6 | (nb 1) | | | 1 |
| Total | (all out) | | 168 | (2 wickets) | | | 40 |

FoW: 1-8, 2-37, 3-57, 4-61, 5-91,   1-3, 2-25
6-118, 7-137, 8-141, 9-165

Bowling	O	M	R	W	O	M	R	W
Trueman	20.3	3	58	3	5	0	28	0
Coldwell	22	3	48	3				
Allen	16	8	22	1				
Flavell	16	3	28	1	4.2	0	11	1
Titmus	4	1	6	1				

Although the First Test had been drawn, the early advantage had gone to England, and in their tour matches against Derbyshire and Yorkshire before the next Test, few of the Australians enhanced their reputation or gave the England selectors anything much to worry about. Even such an experienced campaigner as Sir Frank Worrell had few doubts, with the former West Indian captain writing that 'the Australians have their hands full. The First Test at Trent Bridge was a moral victory for England whose bowling looks far superior and could well have the tourists on the run in the Second Test... England look far better equipped in bowling and the Aussies are certainly up against it.' When the England selectors met up to choose the squad for the Second Test, they therefore had a fairly straightforward task, replacing the injured Boycott with the fit-again Edrich, and with Lord's wicket traditionally assisting the spinners, they also called up Norman Gifford for his Test debut. Initially, the selectors hinted that Sharpe would be omitted, but after the first two days were lost to rain, it was Flavell who dropped out as the selectors opted for the extra batsman. After the weather interruptions at Nottingham, it was frustrating to see the elements interfere again, especially for the English bowlers who were chomping at the bit after their exertions on the final afternoon at Trent Bridge. The MCC were also disappointed by the inactivity, and on the Friday evening they took the rather unprecedented step of asking the Australians if they were prepared to play an extra half-hour each day. It was presented as a gesture of goodwill towards the public, but with the match likely to start in damp conditions that were ideal for the English bowlers, Simpson and his men felt that taking the unheralded step of agreeing to extra time might play into England's hands, and the offer was refused. A few wags had suggested that this was further evidence of negative thinking on the part of the tourists, so when Dexter won the toss on the third morning he invited the Australians to bat first, sensing that the visitors were on the back foot.

There was a real buzz of expectation around the historic ground as the England team emerged from the famous pavilion, and Dexter walked out as the first English captain to send in the Australians at Lord's. The early indications were not good as Trueman's first delivery was a full and very wide delivery that evaded a diving Parks and disappeared down the leg side for four byes. But the Yorkshireman soon got his radar working, and in his third over, he uprooted Lawry's leg stump. He added a fur-

John Edrich (right) goes out to bat with Gordon Barker.

ther four scalps, as the Aussies were bustled out for 176, and hopes of an England victory were given a huge boost. But the home batsmen then found runs hard to come by, as the Australian attack reduced England to 42 for 3. Consolidation was the key word, rather than quick scoring, and John Edrich then made a composed century – his first at international level – to see England to a lead of 70. After his late withdrawal at Nottingham, some critics felt that he owed England a decent score, and on this particular occasion it is unlikely that England would have held the upper hand on first innings had it not been for Edrich's steady batting. As E.M. Wellings wrote, 'John Edrich, short in stature, sturdy of figure, splendidly staunch in spirit, stood firm for England as they panted and puffed their way past Australia's first innings total… He had made his best Test score and the side's Mr Reliable set full sail to the first century of the series as he on-drove Simpson gloriously for the second six of an innings that had been so full of common sense.' The Queen and HRH Prince Philip were present as Edrich reached his maiden Test hundred after 297 minutes at the crease, but with little time left, it was never going to be a match-winning innings. A draw was always on the cards as play began on the final morning, and that is precisely how the game ended shortly after lunch as rain fell again at Lord's, even though the weather forecasters had magnanimously predicted that it would remain dry in north-west London!

England *v.* Australia (Second Test)
Lord's, London
18, 19, 20, 22, 23 June 1964

Result: Match drawn
Toss: England
Umpires: J.S. Buller and J.F. Crapp

Australia First Innings				Second Innings		
W.M. Lawry		b Trueman	4	c Dexter	b Gifford	20
I.R. Redpath	c Parfitt	b Coldwell	30	lbw	b Titmus	36
N.C. O'Neill	c Titmus	b Dexter	26	c Parfitt	b Trueman	22
P.J.P. Burge	lbw	b Dexter	1	c Parfitt	b Titmus	59
B.C. Booth	lbw	b Trueman	14	not out		2
*R.B. Simpson	c Parfitt	b Trueman	0	not out		15
T.R. Veivers		b Gifford	54			
G.D. McKenzie		b Trueman	10			
+A.T.W. Grout	c Dexter	b Gifford	14			
N.J.N. Hawke	not out		5			
G.E. Corling		b Trueman	0			
Extras	(b 8, lb 5, nb 5)		18	(b 8, lb 4, nb 2)		14
Total	(all out)		176	(4 wickets)		168

FoW: 1-8, 2-46, 3-58, 4-84, 5-84, 6-88, 7-132, 8-163, 9-167

1-35, 2-76, 3-143, 4-148

Bowling	O	M	R	W	O	M	R	W
Trueman	25	8	48	5	18	6	52	1
Coldwell	23	7	51	1	19	4	59	0
Gifford	12	6	14	2	17	9	17	1
Dexter	7	1	16	2	3	0	5	0
Titmus	17	6	29	0	17	7	21	2

England First Innings			
*E.R. Dexter		b McKenzie	2
J.H. Edrich	c Redpath	b McKenzie	120
M.C. Cowdrey	c Burge	b Hawke	10
K.F. Barrington	lbw	b McKenzie	5
P.H. Parfitt	lbw	b Corling	20
P.J. Sharpe	lbw	b Hawke	35
+J.M. Parks	c Simpson	b Hawke	12
F.J. Titmus		b Corling	15
F.S. Trueman		b Corling	8
N. Gifford	c Hawke	b Corling	5
L.J. Coldwell	not out		6

Extras	(lb 7, nb 1)	8		
Total	(all out)	246		

FoW: 1-2, 2-33, 3-42, 4-83, 5-138, 6-170, 7-227, 8-229, 9-235

Bowling	O	M	R	W
McKenzie	26	8	69	3
Corling	27.3	9	60	4
Hawke	16	4	41	3
Veivers	9	4	17	0
Simpson	21	8	51	0

The failure of England's batsmen to dominate the Australian attack was starting to worry a few observers, and some members of the Press suggested that the out-of-form Barrington and Cowdrey should make way for the Third Test at Headingley for batsmen who were in-form for their counties. The selectors however felt that it was not worth making wholesale changes just yet, especially when there were still three matches to play in the series, and the only change that they made to the batting was recalling the now fit-again Boycott for his Yorkshire colleague Sharpe. Flavell also replaced Coldwell, while Cartwright, who was enjoying a purple patch with the ball, was included in the twelve, largely as cover for Dexter who had an injured knee and might have been unable to bowl. As it turned out, Dexter was given the all clear, but in the Australian camp, O'Neill was not so fortunate. He was hit a painful blow on the knee by Corling during the warm-up session prior to the start of the game, and was replaced by Cowper in the starting eleven.

Dexter then won the toss, and after the early loss of Edrich, the English skipper treated the Yorkshire crowd to a fine display of batting. As Denis Compton wrote, 'Dexter was batting like a master, and his driving was sending the ball back past the faster bowlers quicker than it had come down the pitch to him!' But Dexter's innings came to an end soon after lunch, and once again, the Australian attack steadily made their way through the English batting, with only Parks offering some resistance, striking some typically powerful blows off his legs, before being caught trying to flick another ball through midwicket.

The next two days of the match at Leeds proved to be the turning points in the series as Peter Burge played a brilliant innings, which not only allowed the tourists to gain a useful lead, but also completely wrested away the initiative from Dexter's men after they had looked like ending up on top after the first innings. The Australian reply had begun with Lawry and Simpson sharing an opening stand of fifty, before Redpath came in at number three, and for the second time in the series showed signs of inexperience. At Lord's his temperament had come into question after he had lost his wicket as the crowd started to barrack him. This time at Leeds he ran out Lawry after calling the opener through for what always appeared to be an unlikely single down to Boycott at short third man. From being 124 for 1 and looking like being able to dictate things, the Australians then stuttered to 154 for 4 as the spinners Titmus and Gifford tricked and teased the tourists during an accurate spell. Sensing that the time was right to have pace at one end, Dexter replaced Gifford with Trueman, and the Yorkshireman immediately came up trumps as he bowled Cowper, who played back to a ball to which he should have gone forward. Titmus then dismissed Veivers and McKenzie in quick succession to leave Australia apparently on the ropes at 187 for 7. Dexter then went for the kill, and took the new ball. But it was a decision that was to cost him dear as Burge, ably supported by the Australian tail, made hay against some ill-directed quicker bowling. Hindsight is a wonderful science, and Dexter came in for some heavy criticism from some sections of the media for opting to go with pace at both ends rather than persevere with Titmus' spin. But many shrewd observers felt that Dexter was quite right in taking the new ball, as his quicker bowlers had seen little action since the morning session, and the Australian tail enders had apparently few pretensions with the bat. But the new ball continued to disappear to all parts of the Leeds ground as Burge and Hawke plundered 63 almost nonchalant runs from 15 overs. In the final over of the day, Burge reached his well-deserved century, but almost as soon as the applause had died down, Hawke was caught at slip by Parfitt.

The following morning, the counter-attack continued as Burge resumed with Wally Grout, with the wicketkeeper lending invaluable assistance as Burge continued the counterattack, as Trueman's opening two-over burst set the tone for the morning session as a further 14 runs were easily added. The spinners were soon wheeling away again, but Grout played them easily, and with Burge in blistering form at the other end, the Australian lead continued to grow. Shortly before lunch, Titmus made the breakthrough as he dismissed Grout for 37, and after the interval, Dexter took the second new ball in the hope of firing out Corling who had shown little aspirations as

Peter Burge.

a batsman so far in the series. However, it was Burge who was the final man to be dismissed, as he swatted another short ball from Trueman straight into the hands of Glamorgan's Alan Rees, who was on the field at deep midwicket as a substitute. Burge departed to plenty of applause from the Headingley crowd who realised that his innings of 160 had tipped the balance in Australia's favour. As Michael Melford wrote in the *Daily Telegraph*, 'in the three hours and fifty minutes since England stood apparently dominant with the seventh wicket having fallen, Burge and his determined aides had added 211, and had completely shattered the moral ascendancy which England had built up with the help of the rain of Trent Bridge and Lord's.'

To make matters worse, Ken Taylor had also been injured while fielding and there were doubts as to whether he would be able to bat. The Australian tails were up, and their bowlers soon capitalised on things as England lost 4 wickets in writing off the arrears, and just to rub salt into the lion's wounds, Parfitt had to retire hurt with a shattered knuckle after being hit by Corling. When play began on Monday morning, the beleaguered English side were only 36 runs ahead, and badly needed a rearguard action. But the Australians were not going to be denied, realising that the pendulum had decisively swung in their favour. Wickets fell at regular intervals, leaving the tourists with a target of 109. Flavell was also out of action with a strained Achilles tendon, so it was Trueman and Titmus who shared the new ball. Trueman soon dismissed Lawry, but Redpath atoned himself for his first innings aberration and guided Australia home by seven wickets.

England *v.* Australia (Third Test)
Headingley, Leeds
2, 3, 4, 6 July 1964

Result: Australia won by 7 wickets
Toss: England
Umpires: C.S. Elliott and W.F.F. Price

England First Innings					Second Innings			
G. Boycott	c Simpson	b Corling	38		c Simpson	b Corling	4	
J.H. Edrich	c Veivers	b McKenzie	3		c Grout	b McKenzie	32	
*E.R. Dexter	c Grout	b McKenzie	66	(5)	c Redpath	b Veivers	17	
K.F. Barrington		b McKenzie	29		lbw	b Veivers	85	
P.H. Parfitt		b Hawke	32	(3)	c Redpath	b Hawke	6	
K. Taylor	c Grout	b Hawke	9	(8)		b Veivers	15	
+J.M. Parks	c Redpath	b Hawke	68	(6)	c Booth	b McKenzie	23	
F.J. Titmus	c Burge	b McKenzie	3	(9)	c Cowper	b Corling	14	
F.S. Trueman	c Cowper	b Hawke	4	(10)	not out		12	
N. Gifford	not out		1	(7)		b McKenzie	1	
J.A. Flavell	c Redpath	b Hawke	5		c Simpson	b Corling	5	
Extras	(lb 9, nb 1)		10		(b 6, lb 6, w 1, nb 2)		15	
Total	(all out)		268		(all out)		229	

FoW: 1-17, 2-74, 3-129, 4-138, 5-163, 6-215, 7-232, 8-260, 9-263

1-13, 2-88, 3-145, 4-156, 5-169, 6-184, 7-192, 8-199, 9-212

Bowling	O	M	R	W	O	M	R	W
McKenzie	26	7	74	4	28	8	53	3
Hawke	31.3	11	75	5	13	1	28	1
Corling	24	7	50	1	17.5	6	52	3
Veivers	17	3	35	0	30	12	70	3
Simpson	5	0	24	0	1	0	11	0

Australia First Innings				Second Innings		
W.M. Lawry	run out		78	c Gifford	b Trueman	1
*R.B. Simpson		b Gifford	24	c Barrington	b Titmus	30
I.R. Redpath		b Gifford	20	not out		58
P.J.P. Burge	c sub	b Trueman	160		b Titmus	8
B.C. Booth	st Parks	b Titmus	4	not out		12
R.M. Cowper		b Trueman	2			
T.R. Veivers	c Parks	b Titmus	8			
G.D. McKenzie		b Titmus	0			
N.J.N. Hawke	c Parfitt	b Trueman	37			
+A.T.W. Grout	lbw	b Titmus	37			
G.E. Corling	not out		2			
Extras	(b 1, lb 8, w 2, nb 6)		17	(b 1, lb 1)		2
Total	(all out)		389	(3 wickets)		111

FoW: 1-50, 2-124, 3-129, 4-154, 5-157, 6-178, 7-178, 8-283, 9-372

1-3, 2-45, 3-64

Bowling	O	M	R	W	O	M	R	W
Trueman	24.3	2	98	3	7	0	28	1
Flavell	29	5	97	0				
Gifford	34	15	62	2	20	5	47	0
Dexter	19	5	40	0	3	0	9	0
Titmus	50	24	69	4	27	19	25	2
Taylor	2	0	6	0				

After the defeat at Headingley, the newspapers were full of articles calling for heads to roll, as the journalists and former players put together their version of an England team that would redress the balance by winning the Fourth Test at Old Trafford, and just for good measure the final Test at The Oval as well. If only cricket was so simple! Many names were being touted, and the result of the selection meeting prior to the Manchester Test was the dropping of Cowdrey for the first time in his international career, as well as Trueman, Flavell and Coldwall, and the selection of an entirely new pace attack of left-armer Fred Rumsey, Middlesex's John Price, who had impressed on

Peter Parfitt hits out while batting for
Middlesex.

the winter tour to India, plus Tom Cartwright, who was the leading wicket-taker on
the county circuit. Gloucestershire's John Mortimore was also named in the twelve-
man party instead of Gifford, while M.J.K. Smith replaced the injured Taylor. However,
it was Smith who was named as twelfth man, as the selectors hoped that an attack of
two off-spinners and four seamers could come up trumps, even though none of the
newly chosen faster bowlers had ever played in a Test match before in England.

For the first time in the series, Simpson won the toss and despite a decent covering
of grass on the wicket, he opted to bat first. The England supporters hoped that he
had made the wrong decision, and crossed their fingers that the new-look pace attack
would utilise the green surface and make early inroads into the Australian batting.
Neither happened, and Lawry and Simpson were largely untroubled in adding 201 for
the first wicket. At the time, it was the highest opening stand for Australia against
England, and ensured that the tourists took full advantage of the placid conditions.
England eventually made a breakthrough, as Lawry was run out again, after another
mix-up with his calling. But Simpson remained unbeaten on 109 at the end of the
opening day, and much to England's frustration, he proceeded to bat right through the
second day as well, ending on 265 not out as Australia's total of 570 for 4 stood like a
tombstone over England's efforts in squaring the series. Although England's bowlers
stuck manfully to their task, Simpson was in resolute mood, realising that by steadfast
application and dour concentration, his innings would ensure that the Ashes remained
in Australian hands. Many people felt that Simpson would declare at the end of day
two – but he decided to bat on for a further fifty-five minutes on the next day, and

Action from the Old Trafford Test as John Mortimore throws the ball to England's wicketkeeper Jim Parks, as both Australian batsmen – Bill Lawry (left) and Bobby Simpson – end up at the bowler's end.

Graham McKenzie.

copped a certain amount of flak from certain sections of the media. Indeed, it was not just the English journalists who got stuck into Simpson, as Sir Frank Worrell wrote 'there is no possible cricketing argument to excuse Bobby Simpson's actions. His side were already insured against defeat, and it was up to him to declare at once this morning and drive for victory. Some sad crimes have been committed against cricket in recent years, which have seriously damaged the reputation of the game. This was one of the blackest and least excusable.' But other members of the press, especially Denis Compton, could not find fault with these tactics, and argued that England would have done exactly the same under the circumstances. As 'Compo' wrote, 'the purpose of the operation was simple and obvious. Simpson was going to grind England into the dust by building such a score that there was no possibility of his losing the match or the Ashes, and so that any deterioration in the weather or the pitch might be in his favour. The tactical thinking was all right. It was the execution that was less than pleasing.'

Whereas Simpson had been in slow mode on the first two days, he quickly went onto the attack on Saturday morning, with a few wags suggesting that he was playing more shots than in both of the preceding days. He duly reached his 300 – the first time a triple-hundred had been recorded in an Old Trafford Test – and appeared all set to go on past Don Bradman's record score of 334. But team glory rather than individual records had always been at the forefront of Simpson's mind, and he spurned the temptation by continuing to attack, until on 311 he edged a wild flail at John Price and Parks' catch ended Simpson's truly heavyweight innings after a monumental 762 minutes of crease occupation. Fifteen minutes after being dismissed, Simpson called an end to his team's innings with their score on 656 for 8 – their fifth-largest total, and the seventh highest in Ashes history. It meant that England needed to bat for the best part of three days in order to avoid defeat, with their first target being the follow-on score of 457. This all seemed a long way away as Edrich fell to McKenzie with the score on 15, but Boycott and Dexter then shared a lively century partnership before McKenzie struck again, as he removed the Yorkshire opener. By the close, England had reached 162 for 2 and their supporters knew that it would require centuries from both of the not out men – Dexter and Barrington – if the follow-on was going to be avoided.

Their prayers were answered the next day as the two men batted throughout most of the day, as England added a further 249 runs for the loss of Dexter, bowled by Veivers after an exquisite innings of 174. Barrington was in majestic form as well, although there was never even the faintest of hopes that his efforts would produce an England win. Instead, it was backs-to-the-wall stuff, and even at the close, with Barrington on 153, England still required a further 46 runs on the last day to avoid the follow-on. These runs were soon knocked off on the final morning, and for the rest of the day, the only shred of interest for the 5,000 or so spectators was whether England would pass Australia's total, and if Barrington would establish a new Test batting score. In the end, the answer to both of these questions was no. By the time England were finally dismissed fifteen minutes before the close of play, they had reached 611, with Barrington finally adjudged leg before to McKenzie for 256, as the Aussie paceman finished with seven wickets to his name.

England *v.* Australia (Fourth Test)
Old Trafford, Manchester
23, 24, 25, 27, 28 July 1964

Result: Match drawn
Toss: Australia
Umpires: J.S. Buller and W.F.F. Price

Australia First Innings					Second Innings	
W.M. Lawry	run out		106	(2)	not out	0
*R.B. Simpson	c Parks	b Price	311	(1)	not out	4
I.R. Redpath	lbw	b Cartwright	19			
N.C. O'Neill		b Price	47			
P.J.P. Burge	c Price	b Cartwright	34			
B.C. Booth	c & b Price		98			
T.R. Veivers	c Edrich	b Rumsey	22			
+A.T.W. Grout	c Dexter	b Rumsey	0			
G.D. McKenzie	not out		0			
N.J.N. Hawke						
G.E. Corling.						
Extras	(b 1, lb 9, nb 9)		19			
Total	(8 wickets declared)		656		(0 wickets)	4

FoW: 1-201, 2-233, 3-318, 4-382, 5-601,
6-646, 7-652, 8-656

Bowling	O	M	R	W	O	M	R	W
Rumsey	35.5	4	99	2				
Price	45	4	183	3				
Cartwright	77	32	118	2				
Titmus	44	14	100	0	1	1	0	0
Dexter	4	0	12	0				
Mortimore	49	13	122	0				
Boycott	1	0	3	0				
Barrington					1	0	4	0

England First Innings			
G. Boycott		b McKenzie	58
J.H. Edrich	c Redpath	b McKenzie	6
*E.R. Dexter		b Veivers	174
K.F. Barrington	lbw	b McKenzie	256
P.H. Parfitt	c Grout	b McKenzie	12
+J.M. Parks	c Hawke	b Veivers	60
F.J. Titmus	c Simpson	b McKenzie	9
J.B. Mortimore	c Burge	b McKenzie	12

T.W. Cartwright		b McKenzie	4
J.S.E. Price		b Veivers	1
F.E. Rumsey	not out		3
Extras	(b 5, lb 11)		16
Total	(all out)		611

FoW: 1-15, 2-126, 3-372, 4-417, 5-560, 6-589, 7-594, 8-602, 9-607

Bowling	O	M	R	W
McKenzie	60	15	153	7
Corling	46	11	96	0
Hawke	63	28	95	0
Simpson	19	4	59	0
Veivers	95.1	36	155	3
O'Neill	10	0	37	0

England's sterling response and Barrington's double-hundred gave a glimmer of hope to home supporters that they might be able to square the series at The Oval. In their quest for a winning side, the selectors recalled Cowdrey, despite the fact that the Kent man had already declined the invitation for the winter tour, while Trueman came back instead of Rumsey as the votes went for a tried and trusted line-up, rather than a more experimental one, in the bid to level the rubber. They also responded to Edrich's indifferent form by dropping the Surrey left-hander and drafting in Warwickshire's Bob Barber, who in the lead up to the Test had scored a century before lunch in the Midlanders' defeat of Australia. Barber was also a useful leg-spinner so his addition allowed the selectors to opt for a more balanced spin attack with Titmus, rather than Mortimore as the finger-spin partner to Barber's wrist-spin.

Their decision looked as if it might be vindicated as, on the morning of the first day, the covers were rolled back to reveal a straw-coloured surface that the experts suggested would increasingly assist the spinners as the match progressed. Then Dexter won the toss, and the England captain had little hesitation in opting to bat first. However, there was low-cloud cover, and in the overcast conditions batting was far from easy, especially against Hawke who returned career-best figures of 6/47 as England were despatched for just 182. But the muggy atmosphere was not the only reason for England's modest total, as some of the home batsmen played strokes that they would want to forget, as they fell in the quest of quick runs. Australia's top order then showed that crease occupation was perfectly possible, and the tourists for the next day or so showed the sort of application and shot selection that their English counterparts had failed to show. But it still remains a moot point whether the term shot selection is an apt one to describe Lawry's five-hour innings. The opener almost eschewed runs at runs and in the eyes of some he could have increased the tempo. But after England had reduced Australia to 96 for 3, it could equally be argued that Australia were best served by their opener dropping anchor. The outcome was a partnership of 106 for the fourth wicket

between Lawry and Booth, with the man from Victoria going on to make a very steady 94. His efforts, while pilloried by some quarters of the English media, allowed Australia to finish the second day 73 runs ahead and still with 5 wickets in hand.

If England were to square the series it was imperative that their experienced attack made early inroads on the Saturday morning, but the omens looked bad at first as Trueman was despatched for 25 off his opening 5 overs by Redpath and Grout. Cartwright typically kept things tight at the other end, but Veivers then came in, determined to maintain the tempo. His forthright approach paid off as the lead was extended towards 150, and a few of the doom and gloom merchants in the press box began writing that England's chances of squaring the series were well and truly slipping away. But a quick rewrite was needed either side of lunch as up stepped Trueman to become the first bowler in Test history to claim 300 Test wickets, as he claimed the final four wickets of Australia's innings. The Yorkshireman left the field to warm applause as Australia ended up 379 all out, with a more-than-useful lead of 197.

The English batsmen knew that quick runs were needed, and Boycott and Barber began in positive vein, adding an assured 80 for the first wicket, with Boycott showing his class with well-timed drives off the front foot, supported by firm punches off the back foot square of the wicket. After Barber was dismissed for ★★★, Dexter maintained the run-rate with a quick-fire ★★★ before swatting McKenzie into Simpson's hands. With Titmus, the night watchman, dropping anchor at the other end, Boycott went on to reach his maiden Test hundred, before Cowdrey and Barrington delighted the fourth-day crowd with some assertive strokeplay. Those who had predicted that the wicket would increasingly assist the spinners were proved wrong as the two Englishmen batted with ease, and by the close they had secured a useful lead of 184. Their efforts set up the prospect of an intriguing final day, but in a series that had begun in damp and dreary conditions, the weather had the final say as a mix of steady

Opposite page: A fine diving catch by Bobby Simpson dismisses Fred Titmus on the final day of the Old Trafford Test.

Above left: Bobby Simpson.

Above right: Fred Trueman.

rain and heavy showers washed out play to leave honours even in the match, and in Australia's favour in the rubber.

As the crowd filed out of a rather dank Oval, they were able to reflect on a series that had never been a classic, or one full of thrilling deeds. As Denis Compton observed, 'the series was a triumph for the defensive-minded. Steadiness replaced hostility with the result that when the weather did not push its nose in, there was not enough firepower to make anything of easy-paced pitches.' But even forty years later, one should not take anything away from Simpson's men, especially when one considers that they had been written-off almost before they had reached English soil, only to leave it with their stock in good order. The reputations of many players were greatly enhanced, and invaluable lessons had been learnt about playing conditions in England, so there were, quite justifiably, many smiles on their faces as the tourists travelled briefly to Holland before heading to Scotland for some exhibition games, prior to departing for India and Pakistan for another round of Test matches.

England *v.* Australia (Fifth Test)
The Oval, London
13, 14, 15, 17, 18 August 1964

Result: Match drawn
Toss: England
Umpires: J.F. Crapp and C.S. Elliott

England First Innings					Second innings		
G. Boycott		b Hawke	30		c Redpath	b Simpson	113
R.W. Barber		b Hawke	24		lbw	b McKenzie	29
*E.R. Dexter	c Booth	b Hawke	23		c Simpson	b McKenzie	25
M.C. Cowdrey	c Grout	b McKenzie	20	(5)	not out		93
K.F. Barrington	c Simpson	b Hawke	47	(6)	not out		54
P.H. Parfitt		b McKenzie	3				
+J.M. Parks	c Simpson	b Corling	10				
F.J. Titmus	c Grout	b Hawke	8	(4)		b McKenzie	56
F.S. Trueman	c Redpath	b Hawke	14				
T.W. Cartwright	c Grout	b McKenzie	0				
J.S.E. Price	not out		0				
Extras	(lb 3)		3		(b 6, lb 4, nb 1)		11
Total	(all out)		182		(4 wickets)		381

FoW: 1-44, 2-61, 3-82, 4-111, 5-117, 6-141, 7-160, 8-173, 9-174

FoW: 1-80, 2-120, 3-200, 4-255

Bowling	O	M	R	W	O	M	R	W
McKenzie	26	6	87	3	38	5	112	3
Corling	14	2	32	1	25	4	65	0
Hawke	25.4	8	47	6	39	8	89	0
Veivers	6	1	13	0	47	15	90	0
Simpson					14	7	14	1

Australia First Innings			
*R.B. Simpson	c Dexter	b Cartwright	24
W.M. Lawry	c Trueman	b Dexter	94
N.C. O'Neill	c Parfitt	b Cartwright	11
P.J.P. Burge	lbw	b Titmus	25
B.C. Booth	c Trueman	b Price	74
I.R. Redpath		b Trueman	45
+A.T.W. Grout		b Cartwright	20
T.R. Veivers	not out		67
G.D. McKenzie	c Cowdrey	b Trueman	0
N.J.N. Hawke	c Cowdrey	b Trueman	14
G.E. Corling	c Parfitt	b Trueman	0

Extras	(b 4, lb 1)	5
Total	(all out)	379

FoW: 1-45, 2-57, 3-96, 4-202, 5-245,
6-279, 7-343, 8-343, 9-367

Bowling	O	M	R	W
Trueman	33.3	6	87	4
Price	21	2	67	1
Cartwright	62	23	110	3
Titmus	42	20	51	1
Barber	6	1	23	0
Dexter	13	1	36	1

Averages in the 1964 Test Series

AUSTRALIA

Batting

	Matches	Innings	Not Out	Runs	High Score	Avg
R.B. Simpson	5	8	2	458	311	76.33
P.J. Burge	5	8	1	322	160	46.00
B.C. Booth	5	8	3	210	98	42.00
T.R. Veivers	5	5	1	159	67★	39.75
W.M. Lawry	5	9	1	317	106	39.62
N.J.N. Hawke	5	4	2	66	37	33.00
N.C. O'Neill	4	6	1	156	47	31.20
I.R. Redpath	5	8	1	216	58★	30.85
A.W.T. Grout	5	5	0	84	37	16.80
G.D. McKenzie	5	5	1	14	10	3.50
G.E. Corling	5	4	1	5	3	1.67

Also batted: R.M. Cowper: 2 runs

Bowling

	O	M	R	W	Avg
G.D. McKenzie	256	61	654	29	22.55
N.J.N. Hawke	242.1	80	496	18	27.55
G.E. Corling	193.1	50	447	12	37.25
T.R. Veivers	228.1	73	444	11	40.36
R.B. Simpson	60	19	159	1	159.00

Also bowled: N.C. O'Neill 10-0-37-0

ENGLAND

Batting

	Matches	Innings	Not Out	Runs	High Score	Avg
K.F. Barrington	5	8	1	531	256	75.85
G. Boycott	4	6	0	291	113	48.50
E.R. Dexter	5	8	0	384	174	48.00
M.C. Cowdrey	3	5	1	188	93★	47.00
J.H. Edrich	3	4	0	161	120	40.25
P.J. Sharpe	2	3	1	71	35★	35.50
J.M. Parks	5	7	0	207	68	29.57
F.J. Titmus	5	8	0	138	56	17.25
P.H. Parfitt	4	5	0	73	32	14.60
F.S. Trueman	4	6	1	42	14	8.40
J.A. Flavell	2	3	0	17	7	5.67
N. Gifford	2	3	1	7	5	3.50
T.W. Cartwright	2	2	0	4	4	2.00
J.S.E. Price	2	2	1	1	1	1.00
L.J. Coldwell	2	3	3	6	6★	—

Also batted: D.A. Allen 21, 3; R.W. Barber 24, 29; K. Taylor 9, 15; J.B. Mortimore 12; F.E. Rumsey 3★

Bowling

	O	M	R	W	Avg
F.S. Trueman	133.3	25	399	17	23.47
N. Gifford	83	35	140	5	28.00
F.J. Titmus	202	92	301	10	30.10
E.R. Dexter	49	7	118	3	39.33
L.J. Coldwell	64	14	158	4	39.50
T.W. Cartwright	139	55	228	5	45.60
J.S.E. Price	66	6	250	4	62.50
J.A. Flavell	49.2	8	136	2	68.00

Also bowled: D.A. Allen 16-8-22-1; R.W. Barber 6-1-23-0; K.F. Barrington 1-0-4-0; G. Boycott 1-0-3-0; J.B. Mortimore 49-13-122-0; F.E. Rumsey 35.5-4-99-2; K. Taylor 2-0-6-0

First-Class Averages for the Australian Tour to the UK – 1964

Batting

	Matches	Innings	Not Out	Runs	High Score	Avg
R.B. Simpson	22	38	8	1,714	311	57.13
B.C. Booth	23	36	8	1,551	193★	55.39
R.M. Cowper	20	29	4	1,287	113	51.48
N.C. O'Neill	20	34	4	1,369	151	45.63
W.M. Lawry	24	41	3	1,601	121	42.13
P.J. Burge	23	34	4	1,114	160	37.13
T.R. Veivers	22	28	7	725	79	34.52
I.R. Redpath	22	37	4	1,075	162	32.57
J. Potter	17	27	3	751	78	31.29
B.N. Jarman	12	17	2	417	105	27.80
R.H.D. Sellers	13	19	8	233	36	21.18
J.W. Martin	16	23	4	361	70	19.00
A.T.W. Grout	18	20	2	303	53	16.83
G.D. McKenzie	22	25	7	290	50	16.11
N.J.N. Hawke	22	16	6	159	37	15.90
A.N. Connolly	15	10	6	27	14	6.75
G.E. Corling	19	13	6	43	6	6.14

Bowling

	O	M	R	W	Avg
N.J.N. Hawke	742	211	1,644	83	19.80
G.D. McKenzie	838.1	217	1,976	88	22.45
A.N. Connolly	323.5	74	850	28	30.35
R.M. Cowper	222.2	59	713	23	31.00
G.E. Corling	575.2	140	1,381	44	31.38
R.B. Simpson	380.5	103	1,033	32	32.28
J.W. Martin	361.1	86	1,134	35	32.40
T.R. Veivers	754.3	226	1,881	52	36.17
R.H.D. Sellers	373.5	93	1,128	30	37.60
J. Potter	140	27	436	11	39.63
I.R. Redpath	30	3	147	3	49.00
N.C. O'Neill	108	21	356	6	59.33
B.C. Booth	24.3	4	106	1	106.80

Also bowled: P.J. Burge 2-0-17-0; A.T.W. Grout 2-0-22-1; B.N. Jarman 3-0-7-0; W.M. Lawry 6-0-32-0

Five Thrilling Contests From 1964

Glamorgan were the youngest of the seventeen counties in the Championship, but following their entry into the first-class game in 1921, they had defeated all the major Test playing nations apart from Australia. But the August Bank Holiday weekend of 1964 saw the Welsh county defeat the Australians for the first time in their proud history in front of a large and fiercely patriotic crowd at Swansea, and all with a side that was missing several regular faces.

The match at the St Helen's ground saw Glamorgan field an eleven that had a mix of youth and experience. Three twenty-two year olds were drafted in, with Euros Lewis opening the batting, Billy Slade in the middle order and reserve wicketkeeper Eifion Jones behind the stumps while young West Indian pace bowler Tony Cordle played as Jeff Jones was rested. But Ossie Wheatley had several regulars at his disposal, including Peter Walker, Don Shepherd, Jim Pressdee, Alan Rees and Alan Jones, and it was the latter who guided Glamorgan to a useful first-innings total after Wheatley had won the toss and elected to bat first on a slow and bare Swansea wicket. Alan Jones drew on his experience of playing State cricket in Australia, and the unflappable left-handed opener dominated the opening partnership with Euros Lewis, before Walker and Rees continued the good work until falling victims to Neil Hawke for 41 and 46 respectively. On the face of it, 197 seemed a modest first-innings total, but a mid-afternoon shower had freshened up the wicket, just to the liking of Don Shepherd and Jim Pressdee. The two spinners proved almost unplayable as the tourists slumped to 39 for 6 by the close of a dramatic opening day's play. Bill Lawry, fresh from his century in the Fourth Test at Old Trafford, was magnificently caught by Billy Slade off Don Shepherd for just 7, and then minutes later Jim Pressdee bowled Bobby Simpson for just 2 – precisely 309 less than the Australian skipper had made in the Manchester Test.

England may have been put to the sword at Old Trafford, but now it was the turn of the Welsh to rejoice against the Aussies, and that evening after play, pubs and clubs throughout South Wales were full of talk about a Glamorgan win and doing something that the English had not achieved. Indeed, there was something of a festive air in Swansea as the National Eisteddfod was being held just down the road from the St Helen's ground, and on the Saturday night and Sunday, the Australian tour party visited the Welsh festival of music, drama and culture. If any of Bobby Simpson's men had been in any doubts, their visit to the Eisteddfod confirmed that the match at Swansea was in effect an extra Test Match against Wales!

There was plenty of Celtic fervour on the Monday morning as play resumed in front of an enormous crowd of around 25,000 that had crammed themselves into

Ossie Wheatley and the Glamorgan squad of 1964. Players from left to right, standing: Alan Jones, Jeff Jones, Peter Walker, Jim Pressdee, Euros Lewis, David Evans, Eifion Jones. Sitting: Tony Lewis, Don Shepherd, Ossie Wheatley, Gilbert Parkhouse, Bernard Hedges.

The cover from a Welsh sports magazine: 'Don Shepherd – The Prince of Wiles!'

every nook and cranny of the famous ground. The atmosphere seemed more like a Welsh rugby international as huge cheers rang around the ground as 'Shep' and 'Pres' began bowling. But hopes of an early breakthrough were thwarted by Tom Veivers who struck a defiant half-century and, mixing caution with aggression, he led a brave fightback with Johnny Martin. Both eventually fell to the Glamorgan spinners, but not before they had seen their side to 101. Despite the tail-end heroics, Glamorgan still had a more than useful lead of 96 on a wicket that was giving increasing assistance to spin, and batting for a second time, Ossie Wheatley's men carefully extended the lead against Veivers' off spin and the skilfully flighted leg-breaks of Bobby Simpson. Tony Lewis and Alan Rees both played little cameos, but Glamorgan then subsided from 126 for 4 to 172 all out, as Simpson finished with 5/33. This left the tourists a target of 268 to win, and in the final ninety minutes of the day it looked as if the Australians would preserve their unbeaten tour record, as Simpson and Lawry launched the run chase with a half-century opening stand. Both batsmen went down the wicket to attack the Glamorgan spinners with some carefully controlled strokes, but with the total on 59, Simpson fell to a fine catch at silly mid off by Peter Walker off Don Shepherd's bowling.

The second day ended with Australia on 75 for 1, leaving the tourists with all of the final day to chase the remaining 193 runs. As far as Glamorgan were concerned, early wickets were essential, and many Welsh prayers were answered in the opening three-quarters of an hour as Shepherd took two wickets, and Norman O'Neill fell to a superb running catch by Tony Lewis. With the Swansea scoreboard reading 92 for 4 Glamorgan had seized the initiative, but with Bill Lawry still at the crease and in typically obdurate mood, there was still plenty of work to be done for the Glamorgan bowlers. For the second time in the match, Tom Veivers then launched a furious assault on the Welsh bowlers, and as the Australian struck a volley of huge sixes, it looked as if Glamorgan's grip on the match was starting to loosen. Lawry and Veivers had added 77 in an hour-and-a-half when Veivers went for one shot too many against Pressdee and was bowled. Wicketkeeper Barry Jarman then gave Lawry valiant support until Lawry, after almost five hours at the wicket, pulled a long hop from Pressdee straight into the hands of Alan Rees at midwicket. Rees took the catch to the accompaniment of an enormous roar, and the departure of a crestfallen Lawry effectively signalled the end of the Australian resistance. Shepherd and Pressdee duly worked their way through the Australian tail with Shepherd in magnificent form taking, in all, five wickets during a marathon spell of controlled off spin. The wily bowler also overcame cramp as he tricked and teased the Australian batsmen, with the

Alan Rees.

final 4 wickets falling for 25 runs. It was Jim Pressdee, though, who took the final wicket as Neil Hawke was caught by wicketkeeper Eifion Jones, with the Australians 37 runs short of their target.

It seemed as if half of Wales surged across the St Helen's outfield as the ecstatic and partisan crowd ran onto the outfield, before gathering in front of the Swansea pavilion to celebrate a great day in Glamorgan's history. But as the champagne bottles were uncorked and the songs grew louder, it became clear that this was not just a victory for Glamorgan, for it was a day which had seen Wales' cricketers achieve something that their English counterparts had not done, and defeat the 1964 Australians!

Glamorgan *v.* Australians
St Helen's, Swansea
1, 3, 4 August 1964

Result: Glamorgan won by 36 runs
Toss: Glamorgan won and batted first
Umpires: W.H. Copson and F. Jakeman

Glamorgan First Innings

				Second Innings		
A. Jones	c Simpson	b Martin	33	c Connolly	b Martin	15
E.J. Lewis	c Simpson	b Veivers	7		b Hawke	11
A.R. Lewis	c Hawke	b Veivers	0	c Connolly	b Veivers	36
P.M. Walker		b Hawke	41	c & b Veivers		9
J.S. Pressdee		b Martin	6	st Jarman	b Simpson	24
A. Rees	c Simpson	b Hawke	48	c Jarman	b Simpson	47
W.D. Slade	not out		14	c Connolly	b Simpson	9
+E.W. Jones	c Connolly	b Veivers	0		b Veivers	4
A.E. Cordle	c Sellers	b Veivers	6	c Potter	b Simpson	6
D.J. Shepherd	c Martin	b Veivers	24	not out		9
★O.S. Wheatley	c Redpath	b Hawke	11	c O'Neill	b Simpson	1
Extras	(lb 6, w 1)		7	(lb 1)		1
Total	(all out)		197	(all out)		172

FoW: 1-42, 2-46, 3-50, 4-62, 5-130, 6-147, 7-150, 8-156, 9-182

1-13, 2-49, 3-67, 4-74, 5-126, 6-152, 7-152, 8-162, 9-171

Bowling	O	M	R	W	O	M	R	W
Connolly	6	1	22	0	3	2	6	0
Hawke	26.1	8	51	3	15	3	30	1
Veivers	28	11	85	5	28	6	65	3
Martin	7	0	31	2	8	2	25	1
Simpson	1	0	1	0	14.1	4	33	5
Sellers					13	6	12	0

Australians First Innings

				Second Innings			
W.M. Lawry	c Slade	b Shepherd	7	c Rees	b Pressdee	64	
I.R. Redpath	c Walker	b Pressdee	6	lbw	b Shepherd	5	
N.C. O'Neill	st E.W. Jones	b Pressdee	0	c A.R. Lewis	b E.J. Lewis	14	
J. Potter	c E.W. Jones	b Pressdee	2		b Shepherd	0	
★R.B. Simpson		b Pressdee	2	c Walker	b Shepherd	32	
+B.N. Jarman	c Slade	b Shepherd	4	c E.W. Jones	b Pressdee	34	
T.R. Veivers	c E.J. Lewis	b Pressdee	51		b Pressdee	54	
J.W. Martin		b Shepherd	12	c Pressdee	b Shepherd	6	
N.J.N. Hawke	c E.W. Jones	b Pressdee	0	c E.W. Jones	b Pressdee	1	
R.H.D. Sellers	lbw	b Shepherd	4	c Slade	b Shepherd	4	
A.N. Connolly	not out		0	not out		0	
Extras	(b 9, lb 1, w 1, nb 2)		13	(b 12, lb 4, nb 2)		18	
Total	(all out)		101	(all out)		232	

FoW: 1-15, 2-15, 3-17, 4-21, 5-21, 6-39, 7-65, 8-90, 9-95

1-59, 2-80, 3-88, 4-92, 5-169, 6-207, 7-217, 8-228, 9-232

Bowling	O	M	R	W	O	M	R	W
Wheatley	4	3	1	0	5	1	11	0
Cordle	5	1	7	0	7	1	14	0
Shepherd	17	12	22	4	52	29	71	5
Pressdee	15.2	5	58	6	28.1	6	65	4
E.J. Lewis					26	13	51	1
Slade					1	0	2	0

The tourists then headed to the West Midlands to play Warwickshire, eager to get back into winning ways after their defeat in South Wales. But the match at Edgbaston saw Mike Smith's team emulate the feats of Ossie Wheatley's side, as Warwickshire, who were resting five of their regular Championship team, won a thrilling game that went to the final over on the third day.

The opening day belonged to Warwickshire opener Bob Barber, who added 97 in even time for the first wicket with Norman Horner, before going on to thrill the 20,000 crowd with a sparkling century before lunch. Neither McKenzie nor Connolly could restrain the Warwickshire opener, whose fine knock reinforced his England aspirations. The Australian spinners also felt the force of Barber's bat, as the twenty-eight year old punished a series of loose deliveries, and peppered the boundary ropes with a series of forceful square cuts and sweeps. He also drove with great force, and one of his powerful blows struck his partner Jim Stewart on the forearm, forcing him to retire hurt. The Australians' out-cricket in the opening session was rather ring-rusty, and met with criticism from several journalists, including the correspondent of *The Times* who wrote that 'it seems palpably impossible that any previous Australian side has bowled so many long hops and full tosses, a happening made worse by the support in the field, where five catches were put down.' Not that the home crowd were complaining, and

Bob Barber.

when Barber reached his century before lunch he received a standing ovation from the delighted supporters. Seven more boundaries flowed from Barber's bat in the opening overs after lunch, but ten minutes after the interval, the rich entertainment came to an abrupt end as he was caught by O'Neill at long on as the Warwickshire man attempted another huge blow off Sellars. He departed with 138 runs to his name – an innings that contained 22 fours and duly resulted in a call-up into the England side.

To some, the rest of the day's play must have felt pretty modest by comparison with the glut of runs before lunch, as Brian Booth, leading the Australians in Simpson's absence, stemmed the flow of runs. After Mike Smith had departed to Cowper for 41, the twenty-three-year-old Aussie added the scalps of John Jameson and Dennis Amiss as the young Warwickshire batsmen tried to maintain the tempo established in the first session. Despite the clatter of wickets, Warwickshire's total of 384 had put them into a healthy position, and for a while on the second day it looked as if the batsmen's efforts might even allow Smith to enforce the follow-on, as the tourists moved from their overnight score of 43 for 1 to 169 for 5 before rain brought a premature end in mid-afternoon. Batting was certainly more difficult than on the previous day, and in the humid atmosphere, only Burge could master the accurate Warwickshire attack, as Jack Bannister and Michael Mence made the ball swing and seam. But it wasn't just the quicker bowlers who prospered, as Barber, no doubt still on cloud nine after his efforts the previous day, pitched his leg-breaks to perfection, much to the chagrin of Burge and Booth, both of whom played and missed several times. Booth was eventually bowled around his legs by Barber, but Burge remained resolute and he was unbeaten on 51 when the weather intervened to bring an early end to play.

Fortunately, the weather was set fair on the final day with the Australians still adrift of the follow-on score of 234, but given what followed later in the day it is debatable whether Smith would have invited the tourists to bat again. As it turned out, Burge dispelled any concerns in the visitor's dressing room by going on to complete his hundred – his first century on tour against county bowlers – and by the time he reached three figures, he had seen his team past the follow-on. The deficit stood at 131, so as soon as Burge reached his hundred, Booth declared, realizing that Smith was keen to make up for lost time and set the Australians a run chase on the final afternoon. Smith duly told his batsmen to go for quick runs, and from 20 overs they plundered 63 for 1 before Smith called a halt and invited the tourists to score 195 in the remaining two-and-a-half hours. Wally Grout had picked up an injury in the field, so Australia were down to ten men, and they began poorly, losing 2 wickets with only 15 runs on the scoreboard. But the tourists remained positive, and forsook shutting up shop by maintaining their pursuit of the victory target. Burge and Potter added 95 in a shade under an hour for the fourth wicket, and in 4 overs after tea, they thrashed the bowling for 31, as Potter struck 3 fours off Roger Edmonds, while Burge deposited Barber's leg spin into the pavilion for six. With half an hour to go, the tourists were 146 for 3, still requiring 49 to win, but Jack Bannister ended the run spree as Burge was caught in the deep. But the instructions from Brian Booth were to still to go for the runs, as Edmonds, a PE teacher at King Edward's School, proceeded to deliver one of the most important spells of his professional cricket career. The twenty-three year old had been roughly treated by Potter, but the young seamer gained revenge as Ronnie Miller held onto a fine running catch at midwicket. The run chase still continued, but fewer boundaries were struck, and as Edmonds stepped up to bowl the final over, the Australians still needed 14 runs to win, with only 2 wickets in hand. Martin clubbed the first ball for four, but then he skied the ball to mid on where John Jameson held onto the catch. Sellers came

Roger Edmonds.

Ronnie Miller.

in and smashed his first ball to the boundary fence, leaving the equation 10 runs from the final 3 balls. Edmonds could have been forgiven for feeling nervous, but he held his composure and bowled Sellers with the next ball as the Australian tried in vain to hit another boundary. Warwickshire had won a thrilling contest by 9 runs and the young schoolteacher received warm applause as he led his team off the field with figures of 5/68 from his 17.4 overs.

When Simpson's men arrived on British soil for the start of their tour in the late spring of 1964, only one county had beaten an Australian touring side since 1912. Now in the space of an amazing week in 1964, Glamorgan and Warwickshire had achieved this feat, and in both cases without many of their regular players.

Warwickshire *v.* Australians
Edgbaston, Birmingham
5, 6, 7 August 1964

Result: Warwickshire won by 9 runs
Toss: Warwickshire won and batted first
Umpires: P.A. Gibb and H. Yarnold

Warwickshire First Innings				Second Innings			
N.F. Horner	c Lawry	b Cowper	42	retired hurt			26
R.W. Barber	c O'Neill	b Sellers	138	c sub	b Connolly		22
W.J.P. Stewart	retired hurt		12				
*M.J.K. Smith	c Potter	b Cowper	41	not out			2
J.A. Jameson	lbw	b Cowper	40				
D.L. Amiss	c & b Cowper		5	(3)	not out		13
+A.C. Smith	lbw	b O'Neill	25				
M.D. Mence	c Burge	b O'Neill	14				
J.D. Bannister	c Connolly	b Sellers	7				
R. Miller		b Martin	26				
R.B. Edmonds	not out		16				
Extras	(b 8, lb 5, w 4, nb 1)		18				
Total	(all out)		384	(1 wicket declared)			63

FoW: 1-97, 2-209, 3-280, 4-289, 5-290,   1-30
6-325, 7-329, 8-343, 9-384

Bowling	O	M	R	W	O	M	R	W
McKenzie	19	2	64	0	6	0	24	0
Connolly	14	1	60	0	9	2	20	1
Cowper	25	4	98	4				
Martin	17	2	52	1	5	1	19	0
Sellers	12	3	68	2				
O'Neill	6	1	24	2				

Australians First Innings

					Second Innings			
W.M. Lawry		b Bannister	12				b Bannister	1
+A.T.W. Grout	c &b Mence		8	(11)	absent hurt			
N.C. O'Neill		b Edmonds	44	(2)			b Edmonds	16
J. Potter	c M.J.K. Smith	b Mence	29	(3)	c Miller		b Edmonds	60
P.J.P. Burge	not out		100	(4)	c sub		b Bannister	53
★B.C. Booth		b Barber	15	(5)	c sub		b Bannister	14
R.M. Cowper	c Mence	b Edmonds	7	(6)	c Bannister		b Miller	18
G.D. McKenzie		b Mence	11	(7)			b Edmonds	0
J.W. Martin		b Mence	5	(8)	c Jameson		b Edmonds	15
R.H.D. Sellers	not out		12	(9)			b Edmonds	4
A.N. Connolly				(10)	not out			0
Extras	(b 4, lb 1, nb 5)		10		(lb 3, nb 1)			4
Total	(8 wickets declared)		253		(all out)			185

FoW: 1-8, 2-44, 3-84, 4-97, 5-146, 6-172, 7-190, 8-202

1-8, 2-15, 3-51, 4-146, 5-155, 6-155, 7-177, 8-185, 9-185.

Bowling	O	M	R	W	O	M	R	W
Bannister	19	3	45	1	11	4	25	3
Mence	18	3	48	4	5	0	27	0
Edmonds	27	7	52	2	17.4	5	68	5
Miller	21	7	57	0	6	2	23	1
Barber	16	4	41	1	10	1	38	0

The County Championship of 1964 also witnessed several dramatic contests, including a topsy-turvy contest at Bristol between Gloucestershire and Nottinghamshire at the end of August. The game began in a quiet manner as Nottinghamshire were dismissed for 245 on the first day, with Ian Moore spending three-and-a-half hours in chiselling out a patient 63. Tony Windows, Ken Graveney and John Mortimore shared the bowling spoils before the Gloucestershire openers, Martin Young and Ron Nicholls, survived the final half-hour in adding 21. On the second morning, Young and Nicholls cut loose as Gloucestershire gained the upper hand, adding 103 for the first wicket, but both departed as Gamini Goonesena caused problems for the home batsmen with his clever variation of flight and spin. The Ceylonese leg-spinner took 5/66 as Gloucestershire were dismissed for 222, giving the visitors a lead of 23 that few could have envisaged back in the morning session. But the pendulum swung back in Gloucestershire's favour as Nottinghamshire batted for a second time, and found life difficult against the bowling of Tony Windows. None of the visitors' top order looked comfortable against Windows' bowling, and as Nottinghamshire slipped to 35 for 5, the home side scented victory. But Maurice Hill and Mike Taylor then played themselves in and adopted a purposeful approach as the shine went off the ball. Nevertheless, batting was still not easy against the persistent Gloucestershire seam attack, and when the visitors were eventually dismissed for 92, it meant that Gloucestershire needed 116 to win.

John Mortimore.

It may have been a small target but the new ball, as in Nottinghamshire's second innings, caused problems for Gloucestershire's top order, and with Andrew Corran and Carlton Forbes both striking early, the visiting bowlers soon had their tails up, reducing Gloucestershire to 46 for 7. But Ken Graveney and Tony Windows then launched a violent counterattack as the new ball bowlers got tired and the change bowlers were introduced. Graveney and Windows added 59 for the eighth wicket to take Gloucestershire within sight of a remarkable victory, and with the clock ticking away, it looked as if the visitors had lost their grip on the contest. But Geoff Millman then recalled Corran and Forbes in a last-ditch attempt to break the partnership. With only a dozen runs needed, Forbes made the all-important breakthrough as he trapped Windows leg before. Corran then repeated the trick against Barrie Meyer, leaving Gloucestershire on 110 for 9 with only a couple of minutes remaining. It looked as if the game would end in a draw, but Martin Ashendon, the young pace bowler, then sliced a ball from Forbes into Moore's hands and Nottinghamshire had won a dramatic contest by 4 runs.

Gloucestershire *v.* Nottinghamshire
Ashley Down Ground, Bristol
26, 27, 28 August 1964

Result: Nottinghamshire won by 4 runs
Toss: Nottinghamshire won and batted first
Umpires: F. Jakeman and H. Yarnold

Nottinghamshire First Innings

J.B. Bolus		b Graveney	14
A. Gill	c Meyer	b Graveney	21
G. Goonesena	lbw	b Windows	4
H.I. Moore	run out		63
M. Hill	lbw	b Windows	30
★+G. Millman	run out		23
N.B. Whittingham		b Mortimore	14
M.N.S. Taylor		b Windows	11
A.J. Corran	lbw	b Mortimore	22
C. Forbes	not out		18
B.D. Wells	run out		0
Extras	(b 11, lb 9, w 1, nb 4)		25
Total	(all out)		245

FoW: 1-34, 2-39, 3-39, 4-90, 5-138, 6-174, 7-191, 8-208, 9-237

Bowling	O	M	R	W
Windows	29	6	51	3
Ashenden	22	5	54	0
Graveney	25	7	43	2
Mortimore	24.2	10	36	2
Allen	17	4	36	0

Second Innings

c Bissex	b Ashenden		3
lbw	b Windows		21
lbw	b Windows		0
c Mortimore	b Windows		5
c Nicholls	b Graveney		23
lbw	b Windows		1
	b Windows		4
	b Allen		13
lbw	b Windows		1
	b Allen		1
not out			4
(b 5, lb 8, nb 3)			16
(all out)			92

1-11, 2-12, 3-34, 4-35, 5-35, 6-56, 7-83, 8-86, 9-88

O	M	R	W
25	12	28	6
5	0	12	1
10	7	5	1
15	9	24	0
12.3	8	5	2
1	1	0	0
1	0	2	0

(Bissex)
(Nicholls)

Gloucestershire First Innings

D.M. Young	c Taylor	b Corran	49
R.B. Nicholls	c Moore	b Goonesena	40
D.G. Bevan		b Gill	29
R.C. White	lbw	b Goonesena	11
D.A. Allen	c Millman	b Goonesena	4
M. Bissex		b Goonesena	8
J.B. Mortimore	lbw	b Corran	23
★J.K.R. Graveney		b Wells	22
A.R. Windows	not out		13
+B.J. Meyer	c Bolus	b Wells	0
M. Ashenden		b Goonesena	2
Extras	(b 7, lb 7, w 1, nb 6)		21
Total	(all out)		222

FoW: 1-103, 2-103, 3-133, 4-137, 5-153, 6-161, 7-195, 8-217, 9-217

Second Innings

	b Forbes		3
c Bolus	b Corran		1
c Corran	b Forbes		3
	b Corran		18
lbw	b Forbes		9
lbw	b Corran		1
run out			5
not out			32
lbw	b Forbes		32
lbw	b Corran		0
c Moore	b Forbes		0
(lb 2, nb 5)			7
(all out)			111

1-3, 2-8, 3-8, 4-35, 5-38, 6-39, 7-46, 8-105, 9-110

Bowling	O	M	R	W	O	M	R	W
Corran	23	9	45	2	20	4	42	4
Forbes	15	4	23	0	18	5	31	5
Wells	33	17	45	2	1	1	0	0
Taylor	8	5	6	0	5	2	4	0
Goonesena	38	11	66	5	4	0	27	0
Gill	6	1	16	1				

The end of season match at Grace Road between Leicestershire and Essex produced another dramatic outcome in the closing overs on the final day. Essex had batted first on the opening day, with Gordon Barker occupying the crease for four-and-a-quarter hours in compiling 146 – his highest score of the season. Brian Taylor and John Wilcox lent useful support by compiling half-centuries as Essex batted throughout the first day to finish on 382 for 9. When play resumed on the Monday morning Trevor Bailey immediately declared hoping that his bowlers, especially leg-spinner Robin Hobbs, would cause problems for the home batsmen on the wearing surface. Events either side of lunch went his way as Leicestershire slipped to 157 for 7, still 225 runs adrift, and with the out-of-form Maurice Hallam as the only recognized batsman remaining, it looked as if the follow-on would be imposed. But Hallam found an erstwhile ally in Terry Spencer, the wholehearted and genial seam bowler, who fancied himself as a forceful lower-order batsman. As Hallam dropped anchor at the other end, Spencer unfurled a range of lusty strokes, striking a couple of huge sixes and fours off Hobbs' leg spin. However, Spencer was fortunate to survive a difficult chance as Bailey spilled a running catch in the deep, and this reprieve seemed to galvanise Spencer who with the resolute Hallam took the score past the follow-on total. Hallam duly recorded his first century of the season, as the pair established a new eighth wicket partnership for the county, beating the previous best of 150 by George Geary and Thomas Sidwell against Surrey in 1926. Completely by coincidence, Geary was on the Leicester

The Leicestershire pair of Brian Booth (left) and Terry Spencer.

Robin Hobbs.

ground that day to see his thirty-eight-year-old record being broken, and the seam bowler also witnessed Spencer confidently passing his previous Championship best score of 75 made against Derbyshire at Burton-on-Trent in 1955. But Spencer soon entered the nervous nineties, and his expansive strokeplay dried up as the prospect of a maiden Championship hundred loomed. But it was not to be, as with his score on 90, he holed out off Barry Knight and the eighth wicket stand ended after adding an invaluable 164 runs. The end of the Leicestershire innings soon followed, leaving Essex with a lead of 44. This was soon extended to over 200 by the second evening as Bailey told his batsmen to score as quickly as possible, in order to give his bowlers sufficient time to dismiss Leicestershire for a second time.

The eventual target of 260 at 89 runs per hour seemed a challenging one, given the way that the Leicestershire top order had disintegrated when batting. Second time around they made a better fist of things, with Brian Booth and Clive Inman sharing a stand of 148 in just eighty-six minutes. For a while on the final afternoon, it looked as if Leicestershire would round off a rather modest season by recording only their fourth Championship win of the summer, but their hopes were thwarted as Hobbs, not in his role as a canny leg spinner, picked up the ball in the outfield and sent in a thirty-yard throw that hit the stumps to narrowly run out Inman for 93. Fifty runs were still needed with 6 wickets in hand, but Hobbs' subtle bowling then accounted for Hallam and Spencer, the two heroes of the first innings, before Bailey came on and in the space of twelve minutes clean bowled Jack van Geloven, Steve Greensword and Ray Julian to leave Leicestershire 19 runs short of their target with only 1 wicket in hand, and just ten minutes remaining. Tom Thompson seemed unperturbed by the situation and he clubbed Hobbs for a mighty six to raise the home team's spirits. But shortly afterwards, he attempted a repeat of the stroke, and for a second or two, it looked as if his blow would clear the boundary, but John Wilcox coolly got under the ball, and held the catch above his head to seal a 12-run victory for Essex.

Leicestershire *v.* Essex

Grace Road, Leicester

29, 31 August, 1 September 1964

Result: Essex won by 12 runs

Toss: Essex won and batted first

Umpires: W.H. Copson and C.S. Elliott

Essex First Innings

Batsman			R
G. Barker	c Spencer	b van Geloven	146
M.J. Bear	lbw	b Spencer	9
+B. Taylor	lbw	b Greensword	65
K.W.R. Fletcher	run out		3
*T.E. Bailey	c Julian	b Thompson	11
B.R. Knight		b Thompson	26
J.W.T. Wilcox	not out		54
R.N.S. Hobbs	c Julian	b van Geloven	11
P.J. Phelan		b Spencer	16
K.C. Preston	c Hallam	b van Geloven	1
C. Hilton	not out		29
Extras	(b 9, lb 2)		11
Total	(9 wickets declared)		382

FoW: 1-23, 2-120, 3-153, 4-199, 5-251, 6-271, 7-299, 8-316, 9-327

Bowling	O	M	R	W
Spencer	26	5	95	2
van Geloven	30	6	108	3
Savage	31	6	88	0
Greensword	11	3	31	1
Thompson	16	4	49	2

Essex Second Innings

Batsman			R
c Inman	b van Geloven		36
c Greensword	b Savage		46
c Julian	b Savage		0
c Greensword	b Thompson		54
c Booth	b Thompson		0
c Jayasinghe	b Savage		0
not out			39
c & b Savage			5
not out			12
c sub	b Thompson		3
Extras	(b 20)		20
Total	(8 wickets declared)		215

FoW: 1-57, 2-59, 3-128, 4-146, 5-153, 6-161, 7-168, 8-176

Bowling	O	M	R	W
	3	0	10	0
	13	1	41	1
	26	6	91	4
	15	3	53	3

Leicestershire First Innings

Batsman			R
B.J. Booth	lbw	b Bailey	26
G.W. Burch	c Preston	b Hobbs	35
J. van Geloven	lbw	b Phelan	2
S. Jayasinghe	c Wilcox	b Hobbs	25
C.C. Inman	c Bear	b Hobbs	0
*M.R. Hallam	c Fletcher	b Hobbs	136
S. Greensword	c Hobbs	b Phelan	5
+R. Julian	c Barker	b Hobbs	0
C.T. Spencer	c Phelan	b Knight	90
J.S. Savage	not out		7
T. Thompson	c Barker	b Hobbs	0

Leicestershire Second Innings

Batsman			R
st Taylor	b Hobbs		81
	b Hilton		26
	b Bailey		2
c Hobbs	b Hilton		14
run out			93
	b Hobbs		0
	b Bailey		2
	b Bailey		5
c Taylor	b Hobbs		8
not out			0
c Wilcox	b Hobbs		7

| Extras | (b 2, lb 2, w 4, nb 4) | 12 | (b 4, lb 4, w 1) | 9 |
| Total | (all out) | 338 | (all out) | 247 |

FoW: 1-55, 2-79, 3-79, 4-90, 5-133, 6-156, 7-157, 8-321, 9-335

1-46, 2-62, 3-210, 4-213, 5-223, 6-229, 7-231, 8-239, 9-241

Bowling	O	M	R	W	O	M	R	W
Knight	13	2	27	1	7	0	36	0
Hilton	18	3	68	0	10	0	44	2
Bailey	14	4	34	1	10	1	25	3
Hobbs	34	8	100	6	10.4	0	69	4
Phelan	17	4	75	2	11	0	64	0
Preston	7	1	22	0				

Perhaps the finest bowling performance in the 1964 Championship came at Hastings in early July as Derek Underwood, the nineteen-year-old left-arm spinner bowled Kent to an overwhelming victory over a lacklustre Sussex team. In the words of *The Times*' correspondent, 'everything in the match was eclipsed by the remarkable bowling of Derek Underwood, whose craft and relentless accuracy, laid Sussex's hopes in the dust.'

Kent had gained the upper hand early on, and they batted throughout the first day to reach 311 for 7 with John Prodger compiling a four-hour century – his first three-figure score of the summer – after Mike Denness had put Kent on their way with an attractive half-century. Their efforts allowed Peter Richardson to declare before the start of the second morning, and as Sussex began their reply, Kent were able to employ attacking fields. Their fast bowlers soon made inroads into the Sussex batting, as the home team's men found few answers to David Sayer's lively pace bowling. Ken Suttle was dismissed early on by a vicious lifter, before the bespectacled Sayer beat Les Lenham for pace and uprooted his stumps. Richard Langridge had dropped anchor at the other end, scoring just 7 in the first hour's play, before finding a useful ally in Graham Cooper. They were also helped by Sayer having to leave the field after breaking his glasses while bowling, and the runs started to flow against Kent's change bowlers, with Langridge and Cooper adding 53 in an hour, before Cooper edged the final ball of the morning session, from Underwood, into the hands of Prodger at slip. Sayer returned in the afternoon session and soon yorked Francis Pountain and Tony Buss to leave Sussex on the verge of the follow-on. This seemed inevitable, as with 4 still needed, Langridge pulled a ball from Peter Jones into square leg's hands. However, John Snow and Ian Thomson played some violent blows to see their side past the follow-on total, and although they were dismissed soon after, Kent still had a very useful lead of 138 on a wicket that was expected to assist the spinners later on.

Some forceful strokeplay by Brian Luckhurst and Peter Richardson saw Kent to 137 for 4 by the close of the second day, and after just quarter of an hour's batting on the final morning, Richardson was able to declare, setting Sussex a stiff target of 301 in the rest of the day's play. But it seemed a generous declaration as Kent's quicker bowlers found little second time around, and were not as menacing as on the previous day. Suttle was able to bat purposefully, while Langridge dropped anchor for a second time in the match. With the Hastings scoreboard reading 22 for 0, Underwood came on and in his first over, he was dispatched for two boundaries by the Sussex batsmen. But the young spinner then struck in his second over as Langridge edged to Prodger at slip, and then two balls later, Lenham completed a sorry match by being held at short leg for 0. But it seemed a very different game at the other end, as Suttle continued to bat with freedom against the other Kent bowlers, and he duly reached his half-century out of 69 on the scoreboard. Underwood started to cause problems for Alan Oakman, who was leading the Sussex side as a result of Dexter's absence on England duty at Leeds, and Oakman was eventually caught behind off Underwood. But the crucial blow was struck at the other end, as Suttle shouldered arms to Sayer, midway through his second spell, and immediately looked around in anguish to see his off stump cartwheeling out of the ground. Underwood promptly changed ends, and in the space of the next hour, he finished off the Sussex resistance. As the effects of the heavy roller wore off, Underwood got the ball to stop and turn alarmingly on the dry and dusty surface, and he proceeded to take 6 wickets for 17 runs in the course of returning career-best figures of 9/28 as Kent won by 145 runs. This was ample revenge for Underwood, who had been roughly treated by Sussex's bowlers the previous summer – his first in the Kent side. Even so, Underwood, still captured 101 wickets in 1963, followed by 101 again in 1964, and during the match with the Australians in front of a packed house at Canterbury, Colin Cowdrey presented young Underwood with his county cap. As Underwood later wrote in his autobiography, 'I had a feeling something was going to happen because Colin, with great thoroughness, had told my parents the evening before that it might be worth them visiting Canterbury the following day. It was no secret ceremony either. It happened soon after the lunch break when we were in the field. Suddenly, Colin held up play, waved in the direction of the pavilion and out came our twelfth man with my

The County Cricket Ground, Hastings.

Derek Underwood.

Peter Richardson.

county cap. Colin made the presentation to me on the field and a packed Canterbury looking on. It was the sort of gesture one had to expect from Colin, and he immediately put me on to bowl!'

Sussex *v.* Kent
Central Recreation Ground, Hastings
4, 6, 7 July 1964

Result: Kent won by 145 runs
Toss: Kent won and elected to bat
Umpires: L.H. Gray and R.S. Lay

Kent First Innings

★P.E. Richardson		b Snow	25	c Thomson	b Cooper	59
M.H. Denness	lbw	b Thomson	58	lbw	b Bell	13
B.W. Luckhurst	c Oakman	b Snow	1		b Snow	48
R.C. Wilson	c Lenham	b Snow	2		b Snow	6
S.E. Leary	st Gunn	b Thomson	39	c Lenham	b Snow	22
J.M. Prodger		b Thomson	102	not out		8
A.L. Dixon	run out		61			
P.H. Jones	not out		11			

Second Innings

+A.W. Catt	not out	0
D.L. Underwood		
D.M. Sayer		

Extras	(b 1, lb 4, w 1, nb 6)	12	(b 2, nb 4)	6
Total	(7 wickets declared)	311	(5 wickets declared)	162

FoW: 1-54, 2-56, 3-78, 4-93, 5-165,   1-44, 2-104, 3-126, 4-137, 5-162
6-286, 7-311

Bowling	O	M	R	W	O	M	R	W
Thomson	27	6	55	3	7	0	30	0
Buss	21	3	93	0				
Snow	20	3	74	3	13.2	2	38	3
Pountain	3	2	8	0				
Bell	22	12	38	0	11	1	47	1
Oakman	12	3	26	0	7	1	29	0
Suttle	5	2	5	0				
Cooper					3	0	12	1

Sussex First Innings				Second Innings		
K.G. Suttle	c Catt	b Sayer	12		b Sayer	64
R.J. Langridge	c Leary	b Jones	89	c Prodger	b Underwood	6
L.J. Lenham		b Sayer	0	c Leary	b Underwood	0
*A.S.M. Oakman	c Prodger	b Underwood	12	c Catt	b Underwood	13
G.C. Cooper	c Prodger	b Underwood	21		b Underwood	25
F.R. Pountain		b Sayer	2	c Denness	b Underwood	11
A. Buss		b Sayer	0	c Luckhurst	b Underwood	18
J.A. Snow	run out		18	c Luckhurst	b Underwood	0
N.I. Thomson		b Sayer	9		b Underwood	6
R.V. Bell	not out		0		b Underwood	0
+T. Gunn	c Leary	b Sayer	0	not out		0

Extras	(b 7, lb 2, w 1)	10	(b 5, lb 6, w 1)	12
Total	(all out, 78 overs)	173	(all out, 56.5 overs)	155

FoW: 1-16, 2-16, 3-33, 4-86, 5-106,   1-30, 2-30, 3-87, 4-91, 5-119,
6-108, 7-158, 8-173, 9-173   6-137, 7-145, 8-150, 9-150

Bowling	O	M	R	W	O	M	R	W
Dixon	14	7	27	0	6	3	10	0
Sayer	21	8	43	6	17	4	50	1
Underwood	25	13	46	2	14.5	6	28	9
Leary	8	2	27	0	14	3	45	0
Jones	4	2	6	1	5	2	10	0
Luckhurst	6	0	14	0				

Grounds for Delight

First-class cricket in Britain today is largely staged at the large, urban headquarters of the county organisations. In contrast, the 1960s were a time when county cricket matches were still staged at a number of picturesque out-grounds in smaller towns and rural settlements. The images opposite show the Crabble Ground at Dover – one of the delightful venues used by Kent, along with a number of other out-grounds including Dartford, Gravesend and Gillingham. But like all of the grounds featured in this section, none of these grounds have been used in the past few years for first-class cricket, as most of the county clubs have centralised their activities at their headquarters.

Like many of their out-grounds, Dover staged an annual cricket week as Kent allocated back-to-back Championship matches to the Crabble Ground. In 1964, the pretty Dover ground was allocated the fixtures against Northamptonshire and Yorkshire in mid-August, but rain rather ruined the first contest, washing out play on the final day when Kent, with 6 wickets standing, needed just 60 runs to win after a fine second-innings spell by Alan Dixon, who took 8/61. But his efforts were to no avail, as the unseasonal weather prevented any play on Tuesday 18 August, and then to make matters worse, the following day the match against Yorkshire began on a pitch that was still quite damp, and with the spinners in their element, the game ended on the second day, with Yorkshire winning by an innings. The eight-acre ground had been laid out on the Crabble Meadows, an area of grazing land to the north of the Channel port, in 1896, and its construction was an outstanding feat of engineering, excavating 38,000 yards of chalk out of the hillside. Opened the following year by Mr George Wyndham MP, the Crabble Ground hosted its first county game in 1907, with the annual cricket week starting the next year.

The Whitsun period saw Kent visit the diminutive Bat and Ball Ground at Gravesend, with games against Surrey and Gloucestershire. Once again, the elements conspired against the Kent club, washing out play on the second day of the Surrey contest and the final day of the Gloucestershire match, and both games ended in draws. The ground dated back to 1857 and was one of the smallest venues used for Championship cricket. Barely three acres in size, even the adjoining tennis courts formed part of the outfield when Championship matches were staged at the ground, and in earlier seasons, straight drives to the boundary only counted as three runs.

Essex were another club to adopt a nomadic existence, moving their tents, temporary seating, mobile toilets and scoreboard van around the county, and calling in for a week at a time at such delightful and quite tranquil places as Chalkwell Park in the coastal resort of Westcliff-on-Sea. The first week of July 1964 saw the tree-lined park

This page: Three views of the cricket ground at Dover.

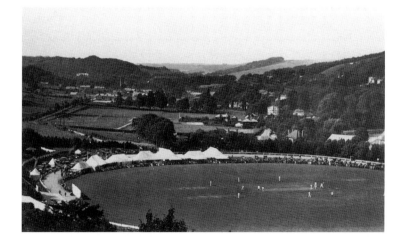

The Bat and Ball Ground, Gravesend.

Chalkwell Park, Westcliff-on-Sea.

host Essex's games against Middlesex and Somerset. Both ended in defeat for the home club, but Trevor Bailey's men nearly won the first contest of 'Westcliff Week' as Middlesex, chasing 213 on a well-worn wicket, slipped to 163 for 7. But Colin Dryborough, the visiting skipper, then played a real captain's innings over the next couple of hours, and his unbeaten 59 saw his team home with one wicket in hand. The cricket ground, laid out in the grounds of the former Chalkwell Hall, had been the venue for a wonderful spell of bowling by Hedley Verity, who in 1936 had match figures of 15/100 when Yorkshire visited the Essex town. The great spinner destroyed Essex with second-innings figures of 9/48 as Essex were beaten by 137 runs.

Glamorgan CCC also used a number of out-grounds in 1964, including Stradey Park in Llanelli – the famous rugby stronghold of West Wales, with the ground having been laid out in the grounds of the former Stradey Castle, on flat meadowland alongside the river Dulais. The cricket pitch and adjoining rugby ground had been created in 1872 and, in January 1887 the Stradey complex played host to the Wales *v.* England rugby international. However, a spell of cold weather meant that the rugby pitch was frozen, so shortly before kick-off a decision was made to switch the contest to the unfrozen cricket ground, and the crowd of 8,000 stood behind ropes that were hastily placed around the cricket outfield. There were far fewer people present at the

A postcard of Llanelli taken in the 1920s, showing Stradey Park in the background.

The Welfare Association ground in Ebbw Vale.

Stradey ground in May 1964, though temperatures were not much higher, as Glamorgan visited the Carmarthenshire town for their Championship match against Derbyshire. The main reason was the dreadful weather that washed out play on the first day, and allowed only 100 minutes of play on the second day. But the rain clouds had disappeared on the final day as the two skippers, Ossie Wheatley and Charlie Lee, attempted to reach a positive outcome. Derbyshire declared at their overnight 45 for 0 before Glamorgan scored a single, thanks to a stroke by Don Shepherd batting left-handed, and then declared after one delivery. Normal service was then resumed as the visitors attempted to set the Welsh side a decent target. None of their batsmen though were at ease against the accurate Glamorgan attack, spearheaded by Wheatley, Shepherd and Peter Walker, and the visitors had limped to 90 for 8 before Lee declared to set Glamorgan a task of scoring 135 runs in two hours and twenty-five minutes. But the wicket remained difficult to score quickly on, and despite the best efforts of both teams, the match petered out into a draw.

The Welfare Association Ground, Ebbw Vale, was another rugby ground used by Glamorgan for their Championship fixtures in 1964. Cricket had been played in the Monmouthshire steel town since the middle of the nineteenth century, with encouragement coming from schoolmasters and various religious leaders who, as believers in

Muscular Christianity, considered that the playing of games helped to give order and moral structure to life within the tightly knit and drink-ridden community. Later, the Ebbw Vale Steel, Iron and Coal Company also realised that it was important for their employees to have the chance to partake in healthy recreation, so in November 1919 they formed the Ebbw Vale Welfare Association and bought an area of land adjacent to a pub. The 'Bridgend Field' subsequently became the Welfare Association Ground, and then from 1973 Eugene Cross Park after the influential and long-standing chairman of the Welfare Trustees. It first staged a Championship fixture in 1946 and at the end of June 1964, the Welfare Ground hosted Glamorgan's match against Warwickshire. The contest proved to be quite a thrilling encounter, and it ended all square, with the visitors' last pair of batsmen hanging on for the draw after they had attempted to chase 215 in four hours. There seemed to be plenty of time available, but Jim Pressdee and Ossie Wheatley halted Warwickshire's progress after they had reached the position of needing just 33 runs with 5 wickets in hand. Wheatley grabbed 3 quick wickets, and after the loss of captain Mike Smith for a well-made 86, Warwickshire's last pair had to mount a brave rearguard action in order to avoid defeat.

The Recreation Trust Ground in Lydney staged Gloucestershire's Championship contest with Derbyshire at the end of July 1964. The ground had first staged club cricket in 1949, with Lydney's cricket club having previously used Bathurst Park, the home of the Bathurst family. The forty acres of land, given to the Recreation Trust by local entrepreneur John Watts and Viscount Bledisloe, the son of Charles Bathurst, had initially been marshland, but after levelling and draining, the wicket gained a

Bathurst Park in Lydney – the home of the town's cricket club from 1946 until the move to the Recreation Trust Ground in 1949.

The Recreation Trust
Ground, Lydney.

Peterborough.

reputation to make it suitable for county matches. The wicket for the match with Derbyshire in 1964 saw Gloucestershire's experienced opener, Ron Nicholls, score a workmanlike hundred on the opening day – his first century since 1962 – and he shared in century stands with Martin Young and Arthur Milton before Ken Graveney declared at the end of the first day with his side on 330 for 7. Derbyshire then batted for the whole of the second day, finishing on 296 for 7, but they fell 10 runs short on the final morning of securing a first-innings lead. With little time available to force a positive outcome, the match meandered to a draw with Barrie Meyer, the Gloucestershire wicketkeeper, taking his pads off to bowl 3 overs in tandem with Martin Young before the umpires called time.

Brian Statham, of Lancashire and England, celebrated his thirty-fourth birthday with a spell of 6/27 as Northamptonshire collapsed dramatically on their annual visit to Peterborough in mid-June 1964. The visitors had earlier batted first and after making 203, a dramatic opening spell from Statham and Ken Higgs saw the home county subside to 31 for 8 before a valiant ninth-wicket stand between Malcolm Scott and Keith Andrew saw Northants avoid the follow-on. However, the match was not concluded, as the weather intervened and washed out play. The Peterborough club ground dates back to the 1830s, with Northants having first visited the ground in 1906. In the mid-1930s it saw two fine performances by the Langridge brothers

Kettering.

of Sussex, with James Langridge claiming 7/44 in 1933, followed by an unbeaten 232 by John Langridge the next year.

In July 1964 Northants recorded a two-day victory over Nottinghamshire at Kettering on a wicket that, like many on club grounds, had a rather uneven bounce. With the ball lifting sharply at times, and then on other occasions keeping low, batting became something of a lottery, and Northants were hugely indebted to Roger Prideaux for surviving for over three-and-a-half hours, and making a gutsy 53. Albert Lightfoot fell one short of a half century, but his third-wicket stand of 100 with Prideaux saw the home team to a useful total of 229 on the capricious surface. It also secured a first-innings lead of 108 after seamer Jim Watts had taken six Nottinghamshire wickets, and with the visiting batsmen offering little resistance second time around, they were dismissed in two-and-a-half hours as Northants recorded a comfortable innings victory. This was Northants' annual visit to the town's pretty ground, lying adjacent to the River Slade, even though Kettering was the place where the county side was born. It was at Kettering on 3 July 1878 when, during a refreshment break in the match between a team of gentlemen representing the north of the county, and a side of amateurs from the south, it was agreed that a representative county team and a formal county club should be formed.

Rain was the only winner at Johnson Park, Yeovil in 1964 as Somerset's annual visit to the town's cricket ground saw their match over the Whitsun period with Northants washed out with only a shade under three-and-a-half hours play being possible. A series of thunderstorms flooded the ground on the second day, and after speaking to the two captains, the umpires had no option but to abandon the game. Yeovil CC had initially played on a ground adjacent to the town's famous Westland aircraft factory, but after the Second World War, the club moved to their own base after Stanley Johnson had generously given £10,000 towards the purchase of twelve acres of farmland adjacent to the

Johnson Park, Yeovil.

Ilchester road, where a recreational complex was subsequently developed for the town's cricketers, rugby players, athletes and tennis players. Used for the first time by Somerset in 1951 it staged 12 Championship matches until 1967

Somerset were blessed with better weather on their visit to the Morlands Athletic Ground in Glastonbury for the Championship match against Sussex in the final week of July 1964. Francis Pountain entertained a decent-sized crowd on the first day with an attractive 96, made in a shade under two-and-a-quarter hours, as Sussex declared on 325 for 9. Half-centuries from captain Bill Alley, Terry Barwell and Colin Atkinson saw the home team then gain a 2-run lead, before off-spinners Roy Kerslake and Brian Langford exploited a wearing wicket. They hustled the visitors out for just 110, and then another forthright innings from Barwell saw Somerset race to an eight-wicket win.

The Manor Ground in Worthing had hosted Championship cricket from 1936 but 1964 saw the final Championship matches held at the venue by Sussex – against Warwickshire and Nottinghamshire. The former resulted in a 182-run defeat for the home side, but Sussex turned the tables on Notts in the second match as the home side won by 114 runs. The first game was a personal success for Ian Thomson who returned match figures of 15/75 but, chasing 206 to win, Sussex subsided in their second innings for 23. None of their batsmen got into double figures as Jack Bannister claimed 6/16, before Tom Cartwright finished things off with two wickets with his only two deliveries of the innings. The second match saw the bowlers prosper again, with Thomson adding another 8 wickets to his tally at a cost of just 51 runs in the match. His efforts saw Sussex gain a 1-run lead on first innings, before Jim Parks made a dashing hundred, and made the visiting fielders pay for dropping a catch from the wicketkeeper early in his innings. Parks was unbeaten on 103 when the last wicket fell, leaving the visitors a target of 208, but they made a poor start against the lively bowling of Thomson and

Morlands Athletic Ground, Glastonbury.

The Manor Ground, Worthing.

The Courtaulds Ground, Coventry.

Snow. The left-armer made early inroads before a fine spell by John Snow saw the young pace bowler take 5/32 as the visitors were dismissed for 93.

The Courtaulds Ground in Coventry staged Warwickshire's match against Somerset at the end of May 1964 and then, later in the summer, their game with Lancashire in the final week of July. Both resulted in good victories for the home team, as Norman Horner with 68 in the first innings and Tom Cartwright with match figures of 9/85 starring in the 70-run defeat of Somerset, before a good all-round team performance with half-centuries by Michael Mence, Jim Stewart and Horner again, saw Warwickshire celebrate a five-wicket victory. The ground was used on a regular basis by Warwickshire between 1946 and 1982, with the county benefiting from the excellent recreational facilities provided by the town's world-famous chemical company.

Dudley hosted Worcestershire's match with Essex in mid-July, but rain rather ruined a contest that saw the seam prosper throughout. Barry Knight finished with match figures of 11/142, but his team were shot out for 121, and had the weather relented the home team were in the box seat 270 runs ahead with 3 wickets in hand. The Tipton Road ground, to the north-east of the town, lay within the shadows of the famous zoo and castle ruins, and staged eighty-seven Championship matches between 1911 and 1971, with neighbours Warwickshire being the most frequent visitors for their West Midland derbies against Worcestershire.

Yorkshire also took cricket around the county, and in 1964 the Anlaby Road ground in Hull hosted the Championship match against Essex. Known as 'The Circle' the ground had been first used by the White Rose club for a county game in 1899, and in 1964 it hosted Yorkshire's opening championship fixture of the summer, against

Tipton Road, Dudley.

The Circle, Hull.

Essex in early May. It was quite a bleak place to start the season, but Yorkshire came out on top after the first two days had seen a cricketing war of attrition, with little to choose between the two sides. But a late burst in Essex's second innings by 'Fiery' Fred Trueman, and then half centuries from Geoff Boycott and Doug Padgett, saw the Tykes start the summer in winning mode as Essex were defeated by seven wickets. The victory at Hull also marked the start of a season that saw, as the following chapter details, Yorkshire do a spot of globetrotting with a transatlantic journey to North America in September and October 1964 – a far cry indeed from Hull!

Yorkshire in North America

A twenty-one-day period in September and October 1964 saw Yorkshire visit the United States, Canada and Bermuda for 12 one-day games. Their party, led by Brian Close, was enhanced by the presence of Gary Sobers, who appeared as a guest player in the final 7 games, and struck a century against the St George's club at Hamilton on the Bermudan leg of the tour. The West Indian also starred with bat and ball in the subsequent matches at Hamilton as Yorkshire ended up unbeaten on their tour, which saw the Tykes record 9 outright victories.

It was the first cricket tour by an English side to North America since before the First World War, and the missionary tour was financed entirely by the Yorkshire club, with the players using their business contacts and friends to raise the £5,500 needed for the visit to go ahead. Ron Roberts, the well-known journalist, was also invited to act as manager, drawing on his wealth of experience of hosting private tours. Indeed, it was Roberts who had first suggested to Brian Close the idea of Yorkshire touring North America. In typically forthright manner, Close replied 'If you can make the arrangements, I'll see about t'brass!' As the arrangements were finalised, Yorkshire secured the backing of HRH The Duke of Edinburgh, who wrote in a letter from Buckingham Palace, 'I have no doubt that the Yorkshire team will have a marvellous time during their tour of Canada and the USA. After the rigours of the County Championship, and the campaign of Test matches, I hope the team will revel in the more light-hearted and variable cricket they will be playing on tour. I send all members of the team my very best wishes for a happy and successful tour as Britain's sporting ambassadors.'

The entire First XI squad, apart from the injured Tony Nicholson, were able to make the tour, with the Yorkshire party arriving in New York in the third week of September at the same time as The Beatles were visiting the north-eastern seaboard. As Fred Trueman later recalled, 'when we got to New York, the scene outside the hotel beggared description. There were more people than I have ever seen in my life. It was like St Peter's Square in Rome on the day of a religious festival, but far more frightening. Almost all of the crowd were on the edge of hysteria. As someone who, for good or ill, is recognised wherever he goes in England, I found it a refreshing change to be somewhere where absolutely nobody knew me.'

After drawing their opening match against a New York Combined Leagues side at Mount Vernon, the tourists recorded their first win of the tour in the next match, against the Combined League side at Randall's Island. Like other matches in the States, the wicket was quite a rough one, and batting at times was a bit of a lottery. After being dismissed for 125, Yorkshire then dismissed the New Yorkers for 56 with Trueman

YORKSHIRE COUNTY CRICKET TEAM-SEASON 1964

AND TOUR DETAILS FOR
AMERICA—CANADA—BERMUDA
TWO SHILLINGS AND SIXPENCE

Clockwise from top:

The Yorkshire side of 1963.

Garry Sobers.

The tour brochure.

taking 6/21. In fact, he might have taken all ten, but for the fact that the ball on count-less occasions beat the batsman and then bounced over the stumps! Fred was in good form the next day as Yorkshire defeated the British Commonwealth CC by the hand-some margin of 304 runs. A century from Ray Illingworth, plus half-centuries from Jimmy Binks and Don Wilson saw the tourists finish on 350, before an opening burst of 4/4 by Trueman, put the home team literally on the back foot, before being dis-missed for just 46.

After flying to Toronto for the Canadian leg of the tour, the Tykes enjoyed the sumptuous hospitality of the Toronto Cricket Club, where they drew their two games against the Canadians, despite attractive half-centuries from Doug Padgett and Geoff Boycott in the first game, followed by John Hampshire and Ray Illingworth in the sec-ond. After the second draw, the team then flew to Calgary where the pre-match prac-tice was stopped by snow, despite the fact that the Yorkshire entourage had arrived in the Prairie town in glorious sunshine. The game with Alberta was abandoned without a ball bowled, and by the next morning five inches of the white stuff had fallen. Then it was to Vancouver and Hollywood for a game with British Colombia and two against South California. All three ended in comfortable victories for Brian Close's men, with Illingworth producing a fine performance with the ball in the first match at Hollywood, before smashing a quick-fire 144 in the second contest.

The team then made another long flight, this time back east to Bermuda for four matches on the Atlantic island. All four resulted in easy wins for the English professionals,

Jimmy Binks, the Yorkshire wicketkeeper.

John Hampshire (left) and Ken Taylor with the Scarborough pavilion in the background.

with Garry Sobers producing a fine all-round performance in the opening game against St George's , taking 4/11 before hitting 117 as Yorkshire batted on after dismissing the home team for just 48. Sobers was among the wickets again in the next match as the Somerset CC were beaten by 31 runs, and then in the penultimate match of the tour, against the Bermudan national team, the West Indian took 4/23 after Phil Sharpe had scored a sublime hundred. Sobers rounded off a good tour by smashing a quick-fire 77 as the Tykes won the final game of the tour, against a Bermudan League XI – their ninth success of the tour. By the time the happy Yorkshire party eventually left Bermuda, they had made twelve night-time flights in the space of a fortnight, and had covered a total of 15,000 miles, but Freddie Trueman was in no doubt that it was the most enjoyable tour he made during his playing career.

Yorkshire in North America: 1964

19 September, Mount Vernon, Westchester
Yorkshire 217 for 8 dec. (D.B. Close 76, Larrier 4/63)
New York Combined Leagues 176/4 (King 56)
Match Drawn

20 September, Randall's Island
Yorkshire 125 (Larrier 6/41)
New York Combined Leagues 56 (F.S. Trueman 6/21)
Yorkshire won by 69 runs

21 September, Washington
Yorkshire 350 (R. Illingworth 103, J.G. Binks 69, D. Wilson 62)
British Commonwealth CC 46 (F.S. Trueman 4/4, D. Wilson 4/31)
Yorkshire won by 304 runs

23 September, Toronto
Yorkshire 251 for 6 dec. (D.E.V. Padgett 77, G. Boycott 75)
Toronto CC 94 for 5
Match Drawn

24 September, Toronto
Yorkshire 189 for 6 dec. (J.H. Hampshire 54, R. Illingworth 51)
Ontario XI 114/2 (A.Khan 52★)
Match Drawn

25 September, Calgary
Alberta *v.* Yorkshire – Match Abandoned

26 September, Vancouver
Yorkshire 246 (J.H. Hampshire 76)
British Columbia 88
Yorkshire won by 158 runs

27 September, Hollywood
Yorkshire 251 (D.E.V. Padgett 50)
Southern California 77 (R. Illingworth 4/17)
Yorkshire won by 174 runs

28 September, Hollywood
Yorkshire 326 for 9 dec. (R. Illingworth 144)
Southern California 65 (D. Wilson 6/11)
Yorkshire won by 261 runs

1 October, Hamilton
St George's CC 48 (G.S. Sobers 4/11)
Yorkshire (after batting on) 322 for 8 (G.S. Sobers 117, G. Boycott 108)
Yorkshire won by five wickets

3 October, Hamilton
Yorkshire 172 (G. Breamer 4/40)
Somerset CC 141 (G.S. Sobers 4/63)
Yorkshire won by 31 runs

4 October, Hamilton
Yorkshire 255 (P.J. Sharpe 114★)
Bermuda 65 (G.S. Sobers 4/23)
Yorkshire won by 190 runs

6 October, Hamilton
Pick of the Leagues XI 69
Yorkshire (after batting on) 167 (G.S. Sobers 77)
Yorkshire won by five wickets

Hail and Farewell

They say that everybody needs a slice of luck in order to succeed, and for Alan Knott, the man who became one of England's finest wicketkeepers, that stroke of good fortune came prior to the start of the 1964 season. At the time, Knott was a junior member of Kent's staff, having originally joined the club as a batsman who could bowl off-breaks. He subsequently kept wicket in second team matches, and what gave the enthusiastic youngster his first taste of county cricket was the decision by Derek Ufton, Kent's regular wicketkeeper, to accept a position as manager of Plymouth Argyle's football team. With Ufton returning to the world of professional football, Tony Catt was Kent's initial choice as wicketkeeper, but then Knott, who had impressed for the county's Second XI and youth teams, was given his chance, against Cambridge University at Folkestone on 27, 29 and 30 June 1964. Knott was thrilled to be given the chance and, as he later recalled in his book *Stumpers View*, 'an added bonus for me was that our long-serving Springbok, Stuart Leary, who lived relatively close to me at Bexleyheath, offered to drive me to the game in his Jaguar. To one accustomed to travelling by buses and trains, and humping kit from ground to ground, that was a luxury. The match will always stick in my mind because it was very close and exciting, and I was fortunate enough to make the winning hit off Graham Pritchard in the final over.'

His nimble-footed performances led to his selection on the International Cavaliers tour to the West Indies in the winter of 1964/65, and after returning from the Caribbean, Knott became Kent's regular wicketkeeper. He soon developed an almost innate understanding with left-arm spinner Derek Underwood, and it was not long before the entry 'c Knott b Underwood' became a common sight on the county's scorecards. In 1967 he made his Test debut, playing for England in the Second Test against Pakistan at Trent Bridge. This was the first of 95 England caps as Knott enjoyed a glittering career at international level with the Kent man establishing a host of new wicketkeeping records. Highly superstitious and a fitness fanatic, Knott worked hard on his agility and Knott's callisthenics and leg stretches were a familiar sight in between deliveries. He eventually retired at the end of the 1985 season with 1,211 catches and 133 first-class stumpings to his name.

Graham Roope made his first-class debut for Surrey in 1964, making 4 against Warwickshire at The Oval in the final game of the season. It may not have been the most successful of starts for the tall and raw-boned youngster from Bradfield College, but he had impressed the county's coaching staff with his correct and deft strokeplay for the county's Second XI, as well as some accurate in-swing bowling. He reappeared once in 1965, and then from the middle of the 1966 season Roope got an extended

Alan Knott.

Graham Roope.

run in the First XI, and had the chance to display his all-round talents. Roope duly blossomed into a talented right-handed batsman, a useful medium-fast bowler and a highly dependable fielder close to the wicket, especially at second slip, where he held a number of brilliant catches as the Surrey seam attack scythed their way through opposition batting. He went on to win 21 Test caps for England between 1973 and 1978, and his reputation as a safe pair of hands in the slips often swayed the selectors' vote in his favour over other equally good county batsmen. His finest hour in England colours came quite fittingly on his home ground at The Oval in 1975 when the Surrey man made a solid 77 that helped to save the game for his side against the fiery Australian pace attack of Lillee and Thomson. Although he never recorded a Test century, 7 half-centuries and 35 catches bear testament to both his abilities as a cricketer and his steely determination and fierce competitive instincts. He gave loyal service to Surrey before retiring in 1982 with 19,116 first-class runs and 225 wickets to his name.

Roger Davis, who made his first appearance for Glamorgan in 1964, had two brushes with fame on the cricket field. The first came at Swansea in 1968 during the Welsh county's match against Nottinghamshire at Swansea when Garry Sobers, the great West Indian all-rounder, became the first man in cricket history to score six sixes in an over, hitting Glamorgan's Malcolm Nash for 36 in the space of six deliveries as his side moved towards a declaration. Nash's normal style was left-arm seam, and Davis was usually one of the fielders close to the bat. On this occasion, Nash was

Roger Davis.

experimenting with slow left-arm, and as the historic over began, Davis found himself standing on the long-off boundary in front of the steep terraces that led up to the St Helen's pavilion. After hitting the first 4 balls for six, Sobers lofted one high in the air, straight towards Davis. But as the twenty-two year old gleefully held on to the ball, he fell backwards over the ropes, and a long consultation took place between the umpires to ascertain whether Davis had safely caught the ball inside the playing area. Eventually a six was signalled, and Sobers proceeded to savagely pull the next ball clean out of the ground, and to create a name for himself in the cricket record books. On the second occasion when Davis' name hit the headlines, it nearly resulted in the Glamorgan all-rounder losing his life on the cricket field. The incident came in 1971 during the Championship match with Warwickshire at Cardiff as Davis was struck a sickening blow on the side of his head while fielding at short leg. These were the days when the only thing that fielders wore for protection was a box, and as soon as he was hit on the head, Davis collapsed to the ground, and went into convulsion. Thankfully, he was given the kiss of life by a doctor who ran onto the Sophia Gardens ground from the members enclosure, and after a short spell in hospital, Davis made a full recovery, and returned to the Glamorgan side the following year. The former Blundell's schoolboy made his first county appearance aged eighteen against Kent at Cardiff Arms Park on 29 August 1964. He soon developed into a sound and cool-headed middle-order batsman and accurate off spin bowler. Later in his career, Roger moved up to open the batting with Alan Jones. Despite his near-fatal accident, Davis was a brilliant fielder close to the wicket, and he took many outstanding catches. Indeed, his agile and brave fielding was one of the vital ingredients in Glamorgan winning the County Championship in 1969.

Ken Shuttleworth.

1964 saw the first appearance in the Lancashire side of Ken Shuttleworth. The county was well blessed with seam bowlers at the time, and it spoke volumes for Shuttleworth's rich potential that he was able to force his way into the team for 6 Championship matches. Despite many opportunities, Shuttleworth never fully fulfilled this early promise, and although he won 5 Test caps, his career never really took off in the way that the people who first saw the tall, dark-haired bowler in county cricket in 1964 had anticipated. Shuttleworth had an approach to the wicket that was long enough to draw favourable comparison with Brian Statham, and his side-on action and long delivery stride was very reminiscent of Fred Trueman. He never quite matched these great bowlers' feats, but at his peak, Shuttleworth was deceptively quick and he could surprise even the most experienced of county batsmen with his sharp out-swing.

He eventually established a regular spot in the Lancashire side during the 1968 season, and that summer he recorded career-best figures of 7/41 against Essex. The following year, his name started to be mentioned as a future Test bowler, and in 1970 he made his first appearance for England in their unofficial international match against the Rest of the World. At the end of the summer, he won selection for the 1970/71 MCC tour to Australia, and he was a member of Ray Illingworth's team that won the Ashes. Shuttleworth made his Test debut in the opening match of the rubber at Brisbane, and he took 5/47 in Australia's second innings. After the team's triumphant return from Down Under, Shuttleworth played in just one Test on English soil, appearing at Edgbaston in the First Test of the series against Pakistan. But as he became older, Shuttleworth became increasingly hampered by a variety of niggling ailments, and in 1976 he left Lancashire and joined Leicestershire, where he continued to enjoy

Clive Radley, standing second from the right, with the Middlesex team of 1969. From left to right, standing: M.J. Smith, J.S.E. Price, A.N. Connolly, K.V. Jones, C.T. Radley, H.C. Latchman. Sitting: R.W. Hooker, J.T. Murray, P.H. Parfitt, F.J. Titmus, W.E. Russell.

moments of success, with his steady seam bowling as well as his lusty and at times flamboyant tail-end hitting.

For the opening match of the 1964 season against Cambridge University at Fenner's, Middlesex included in their team a stocky nineteen-year-old batsman called Clive Radley. Born in Hertford, and educated in Norwich, he had arrived at Lord's via the same Norfolk–Middlesex route that had been followed by Bill Edrich and Peter Parfitt. Although he did not get a chance to bat on his debut, Radley got further opportunities during the summer to prove that one day he also might follow in Edrich's and Parfitt's steps and represent England. No-one who saw Radley in the following years would ever claim that he was the most elegant or graceful of batsmen. But few would find fault with his phenomenal application, gritty determination and unflappable temperament – talents that saw Radley become a highly accomplished and consistent member of Middlesex's top order, and helped him share in a record sixth-wicket stand of 227 with Fred Titmus against the 1965 South Africans at Lord's.

Radley's approach to batting was uncomplicated and simple – get quickly into line, watch the ball and play within your limitations. So for season after season between 1964 and 1987 Radley grafted away and passed 1,000 runs on sixteen occasions. He also developed a knack of infuriating opponents by gently placing the ball into unguarded parts of the field and then, with great glee, scampering a quick single. These hastily run singles, plus an ability to improvise, meant that Radley became an integral part of Middlesex's one-day team that won five limited-overs trophies between 1977 and 1986. It was also no coincidence that during this time, Middlesex won the Championship five times and shared it on another occasion. Higher honours came late to Radley, and he was approaching his thirty-fourth birthday when he made his England debut at Christchurch against New Zealand in the Second Test of the 1977/78 MCC tour. Despite now wearing the lion and three crowns on his chest, Radley did not change his approach to batting, and he concentrated on what he knew best, and what had served him so well since his county debut in 1964. In his second Test appearance he occupied the crease at Auckland for almost eleven hours in making 158, and on his return to the UK in 1978 he took a hundred off the Pakistan attack at Edgbaston. His England career ended at the end of the summer, but by that time Radley had amassed a healthy Test average of 48.10, and in his 8 appearances at international level, he never once ended up on the losing team.

In 1964 Barry Wood made five appearances for Yorkshire, with his county debut coming at Middlesbrough on 6 June However, the combative and gutsy all-rounder subsequently found few opportunities with his native county, so in 1966 he moved across the Pennines to join Lancashire. It proved to be a wise move as he won his county cap in 1968 and developed into a tough and uncompromising opening batsman. He relished the challenge of facing fast bowling and what Wood, at a fraction under 5'7", may have lacked in height, he more than made up for in heart, fiercely hooking and savagely pulling anything that the opposing quicks sent his way in the hope of unsettling him. His slow-medium swing bowling was highly effective in overcast conditions and his abilities to contain opposing batsmen were highly valued in one-day matches. As befitted a fierce competitor, he loved the challenge that

Barry Wood – seen here in 1982 when he was captain of Derbyshire.

bowling presented in limited-overs games, and he enjoyed much success in the role of all-rounder as Lancashire became the one-day kings of the early 1970s. Wood's personal share of glory included six Man of the Match awards in the Gillette Cup, plus a further eleven Gold Awards in the Benson & Hedges Cup. In 1972 Wood made the first of twelve appearances in Tests for England in the final Test of the Ashes series, and in the second innings of his first Test it looked as if he would mark his debut with a century, as he frequently drove the ball to The Oval boundary. But he was 10 runs short of this landmark when he was finally trapped leg before. His efforts won him a place on the winter tour to the sub-continent, but he looked less at ease against the wily Indian spinners, and his subsequent appearances at international level were sporadic. After a highly successful Benefit year with Lancashire in 1979, Wood joined Derbyshire and he subsequently led them for the next two seasons, including their NatWest Trophy triumph in 1981.

Not many seventeen-year-old bowlers can claim to have taken a wicket in their first over of county cricket, but that is precisely what Pat Pocock, the young Surrey off-spinner, did on his first-class debut on 1 August 1964, playing against Nottinghamshire at The Oval. The youngster entered the attack before lunch and with his first five deliveries, to Nottinghamshire's number four Ian Moore, he did not concede a run, but then his sixth delivery saw Moore edge the ball to Stewart Storey at slip to give the youngster his first county victim and a wicket maiden to boot. Pocock continued for two hours after the interval, and despite being struck for six, he had the commendable figures of 3/68 when an attack of cramp saw the young spinner leave the field for treatment.

Pocock was one of a number of promising youngsters blooded by Surrey during 1964. Born in Bangor, but brought up in South London, he appeared in a further eight Championship games and impressed with his smooth, high and classical side-on action. Right from these early days, the gauche youngster proved to be a big spinner of the ball, with a deceptive, dipping flight. As he gained in further experience, the following seasons saw 'Percy' add a number of subtle variations to his armoury, and all without losing his prime asset of sharp spin. Indeed, throughout his career, which lasted until 1986, Pocock became known as a spinner who was always prepared to experiment with changes of grip, angle, flight and pace. In the winter of 1967/68, Pocock was included in England's party for the tour to the Caribbean, and the boating accident that led to Fred Titmus losing four toes resulted in Pocock's swift promotion into the world of international cricket. He made his Test debut in the Third Test against the West Indies at Bridgetown, and then in the opening Test of the 1968 Ashes series Pocock claimed 6/79. Despite his success in this game, and continued success at county level, this proved to be Pocock's only appearance against Australia in Test cricket. Even though he played well on England's tours to India, Pakistan and the Caribbean, Pocock did not play in another Test on English soil until the 1976 series against the West Indies. He was only given two chances before being discarded again, and remaining in the international wilderness until returning at the age of thirty-seven in the series against the 1984 West Indians. He drew on all of his experience to contain the gifted Caribbean strokemakers, and he then played a crucial part in England's successful tour of India in 1984/85. It proved to be a wonderful postscript to the career of a most wholehearted and enthusiastic cricketer.

Mike Harris.

'Pasty' Harris made his debut in first-class cricket on 6 May 1964 as Middlesex played Oxford University at The Parks. The young Cornishman had played some impressive innings for the MCC ground staff, and on his first-class bow, 'Pasty' made an assured 35 before being bowled by his namesake Christopher Harris, the Oxford seamer His promising performance at Oxford led to his Championship debut the following week when Worcestershire visited Lord's. After a further five Championship appearances in 1965, the right-hander secured a regular berth in the Middlesex side in 1966, and then the following year Harris amassed 1,715 runs and hit four centuries. But after this dramatic breakthrough, his batting form rather nose-dived, as in 1968 he made just 560 runs from twenty-seven innings, revealed something of a weakness on the back foot, and lost his place in the Middlesex side. In 1969 Harris moved to Nottinghamshire. The change of county certainly did the trick as he immediately returned to form, completing a thousand runs in 1969 before enjoying a wonderful summer in 1971, making 2,238 runs at an average of 50.86. He struck 9 centuries for Nottinghamshire, and on two occasions – against Leicestershire at Grace Road, and Essex at Chelmsford – Harris struck a century in both innings of the match. Harris gave over a decade of good service to Nottinghamshire, largely as an opening batsman, as well as keeping wicket in one-day matches. He retired at the end of 1982 having scored 19,196 first-class runs and recording 41 centuries, before becoming a first-class umpire, joining the reserve list in 1988, and then being elevated to the first-class list in 1998.

Left: Neal Abberley.

Opposite: Gilbert Parkhouse, sitting far left, with other members of the Glamorgan team of 1951. From left to right, standing: W.E. Jones, P.B. Clift, N.G. Hever, J.E. McConnon, D.J. Shepherd, B.L. Muncer, J.E. Pleass. Sitting: W.G.A. Parkhouse, H.G. Davies, W. Wooller, D.E. Davies, A.J. Watkins.

1964 saw another county stalwart play his first county innings, as on 13 May Neal Abberley made his first-class debut for Warwickshire. It also began an association with the West Midlands club that has seen the popular Birmingham-born batsman move from being a first-team regular to second-team captain, and latterly coach and manager of Edgbaston's indoor cricket school. It was quite a successful debut for the young Warwickshire batsman, as he top-scored with 54 in Warwickshire's first innings. But despite this rich promise, he did not appear again in the county's first team for over a year, but this time he earned an extended run in the team, and the following summer he secured a regular berth in the team, and enjoyed a fruitful summer that culminated in a career-best 117★ against Essex at Edgbaston. He also won selection on the MCC Under-25 tour to Pakistan in 1966/67, and on his first appearance against Central Zone the Warwickshire opener made a well-composed 92. However, he also quite badly injured his hand during the game, and this forced him to miss the rest of the tour, and the injury also continued to affect his batting for the next few years.

Abberley had built up a reputation as a forceful batsman in League cricket, and the introduction of an increasing amount of limited-overs cricket from 1969 onwards gave a further boost to Abberley's career. His natural aggression was a great asset to the team, and he always kept the scoreboard moving with a series of subtle dabs and cuts. He was also a good enough batsman to score a fine 113★ against Hampshire at Bournemouth in their Benson & Hedges Cup tie in 1976. His efforts helped Warwickshire win the game by 45 runs, and for his efforts he deservedly won the Gold Award.

1964 saw the end of Gilbert Parkhouse's illustrious career with Glamorgan. Since 1948 he had delighted the Welsh county's supporters with his elegant and stylish strokeplay. By the time he left the county game in 1964, Parkhouse had over 23,000 runs in first-class cricket to his credit, and among the many records he set was becoming the first (and so far only) Glamorgan batsman to have scored Championship centuries against every first-class county. Parkhouse had enjoyed a wonderful first year on the county circuit in 1948 as he scored over a thousand runs in his debut season and was a member of the Glamorgan side that won the county title for the first time in the club's history. Two years later he moved up to the world of international cricket after making his England debut in their series with the 1950 West Indies. His fine form at county level resulted in his selection on the England tour to Australia and New Zealand in 1950/51, but he subsequently struggled with poor health on the tour and despite playing in three Tests, he never really gave a proper account of his true abilities. Although he continued to be one of the most consistent and attractive batsmen on the county circuit, it wasn't until 1959 that Parkhouse's services were called upon again by the England selectors. 1959 proved to be a magnificent season for the Swansea-born batsman, as he amassed a club record of 2,071 runs, and this sheer weight of runs led to Parkhouse being recalled to the England side for the Third and Fourth Tests against India. During the early 1960s, Parkhouse started to be affected by a series of niggling back injuries. These eventually resulted in him retiring from county cricket in 1964 to take up a post as coach with Worcestershire. He helped them retain the county title in 1965, before moving to Scotland where he was cricket coach at Stewarts-Melville College in Edinburgh from 1966 until 1987.

Sam Cook was another veteran to call it a day in 1964 after a wonderful career as a left-arm spinner with Gloucestershire that had seen the 'Tetbury Twirler' claim 1,768 wickets for the West Country side as well as appearing in one Test for England in their 1947 series against the Springboks. Cook had burst onto the county circuit in 1946, taking a wicket with his first ever ball for Gloucestershire, against Oxford University at The Parks. Wally Hammond had been mightily impressed with the twenty-four year old, who had been recommended to pursue a career with the county after some fine performances in Services cricket. After seeing Cook in the nets at Bristol, Hammond told a watching official, 'I reckon this fellow will take 100 wickets this year and I think that he will play for England one day.' Hammond was right on both counts, as Cook finished the 1946 season with 113 Championship victims, and then the following year, after impressing for the MCC against the South Africans, Cook was called up for the First Test at Trent Bridge. Not everyone though thought that Cook should play – his county colleague, Tom Goddard, quietly told him that he should not even think about playing for England at Nottingham as the wicket had a reputation of being a feath-erbed. Perhaps Cook should have listened to the sage words of the experienced Goddard, as he found the wicket very docile, and in an attempt to secure a wicket, Cook tried too hard and lost his customary accuracy. He finished with figures of 0-127 from 30 overs, and was replaced by Kent's Doug Wright for the Second Test. The loyal and phlegmatic Cook never got another chance at Test level, and to a large extent he was very unlucky to be at the peak of his game at a time when England could call up upon the likes of Jack Young, Johnny Wardle and Tony Lock. Many infe-rior spinners have subsequently won the England cap – several of whom appeared while Sam was a first-class umpire, standing in 297 games between 1965 and 1986 But Cook was never a bitter man, and instead his down-to-earth outlook meant that he held a very pragmatic outlook on life, never moaning about his misfortunes at Test level, or bearing grudges against the England selectors. In fact, the acclaim of winning an England cap rather embarrassed him, and instead of talking about what might have been at international level, Cook was perfectly content to take a regular bag of wick-ets for Gloucestershire, and then sit down after the day's play for a pint or two.

Martin Young was another Gloucestershire cricketer to leave the first-class game at the end of the 1964 season. Some felt that his decision to retire was rather premature, especially after the way the previous summer he had treated the West Indian fast bowlers with complete disdain in scoring 127 against the tourists at Bristol. His efforts laid to rest once and for all a feeling that Young was never at his best against genuine quick bowling. His sparkling batting also drew fulsome praise from Frank Worrell, the West Indian captain, and he echoed the thoughts of many Gloucestershire supporters when at the end of the game he said 'Why isn't Young in the England side?'

Young had first joined Gloucestershire in 1949 after a brief spell on the Worcestershire staff. The first of his 40 first-class centuries occurred the following year against his former employers, and in this, his first full season of Championship crick-et, he scored 1,558 runs. He subsequently became a consistent and reliable opening batsman, with an unflappable temperament, rock-solid technique and a wide array of strokes, especially through the off side. On two occasions, Young amassed over 2,000

Sam Cook.

Martin Young.

runs in a season – he reached this landmark in 1955 and 1959, and on both occasions he was part of a highly productive opening partnership with Arthur Milton. These fine efforts led to his name being touted as a possible England opener, but international honours never came his way, even though he remained one of the game's most attractive and dependable opening batsmen. Like his colleague Sam Cook, Young was unlucky to be playing at a time when England were well blessed with many fine opening batsmen. Throughout his career, Young remained very much a gentleman cricketer, with his immaculate and perfectly timed off drives matching his dapper dress sense and sophisticated manner . After enjoying a successful Benefit year in 1963, Young played his final game for Gloucestershire against Yorkshire at Bristol in September 1964, before emigrating to South Africa where he became a highly successful sports broadcaster and journalist.

In September 1964, Ken Preston played his final Championship match for Essex, against Leicestershire at Grace Road. The fast bowler failed to take a wicket in his final first-class appearance, and his departure from the county game was in stark contrast to his arrival back in 1948 when his hostility saw him take the wicket of Glamorgan's Phil Clift in just his third over on his county debut at the Arms Park ground in Cardiff. Further sparkling performances in 1948 marked out the fast bowler as someone to follow in 1949, but he broke a leg playing football during the winter months, and Preston's hostile fast bowling was not seen again until 1950. When he returned, he shortened his run-up and reduced his pace, preferring instead to bowl at fast-medium pace, with a quite lethal leg-cutter. It proved to be a wise move as it prolonged his career in the county game, and even in the late 1950s he could easily deliver prolonged spells of quite lethal seam bowling. In 1956 he took career-best figures of 7/55 against

Ken Preston.

Northamptonshire at Peterborough, and then the following summer he enjoyed his best summer as he claimed a total of 140 wickets at a fraction over 20 runs apiece. Even in the early 1960s Preston could be a handful and in 1962 he recorded his best match analysis – 12/85 against Lancashire at Leyton. Two years later he bade farewell to the county game and took up a position as cricket coach and manager of the school shop at Brentwood School.

Bibliography

Quotations and extracts were drawn from the following books:

Ken Barrington, *Playing it Straight* (Stanley Paul, 1968).
Geoff Boycott, *Put to the Test* (Arthur Barker, 1979).
Mike Brearley, *The Art of Captaincy* (Hodder and Stoughton, 1985).
Denis Compton, *Denis Compton's Test Diary* (Nicholas Kaye, 1964).
Ted Dexter, *Ted Dexter Declares* (Stanley Paul, 1966).
Tom Graveney, *Cricket Over Forty* (Pelham Books, 1970).
Alan Knott, *Stumper's View* (Stanley Paul, 1972).
John Snow, *Cricket Rebel* (Hamlyn, 1976).
Fred Trueman, *The Freddie Trueman Story* (Stanley Paul, 1965) and *Fast Fury* (Stanley Paul, 1961).
Derek Underwood, *Beating the Bat* (Stanley Paul, 1975).

Other quotes came from match reports and articles in *The Times*, *The Daily Telegraph*, *Sunday Express*, *Sunday Mirror*, *Playfair Cricket Monthly*, *The Evening Standard* and the *Wisden Cricketers' Almanac* for 1965

Index

Other titles published by Tempus

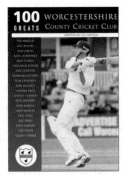

Worcestershire CCC 100 Greats
LES HATTON

Many wonderful players and characters have represented Worcestershire CCC over the decades since its founding in the nineteenth century – men such as H.K. Foster, Don Kenyon, Tom Graveney and Graeme Hick. This book, comprising biographies, illustrations and statistics, celebrates the acheivements of 100 of the county's all-time greats. Compiled by club statistician Len Hatton, it will delight anyone with an interest in Worcestershire cricket.
0 7524 2194 8

Victory England's Greatest Modern Test Wins
ALAN BONE with a foreword and commentary by CHRISTOPHER MARTIN-JENKINS

The England team has delighted and frustrated in equal measures over the past few decades. This book highlights the most memorable occasions on which the side has triumphed, be it a consummate thrashing of the opposition or an epic comeback from the brink of defeat. With a foreword and commentary from the inimitable Christopher Martin-Jenkins, this book will be a source of nostalgia and delight for all England cricket fans.
0 7524 3415 2

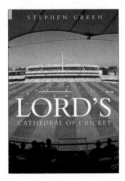

Lord's Cathedral of Cricket
STEPHEN GREEN

The history of the greatest and most evocative sports ground in the world. Lord's: Cathedral of Cricket charts the history of the ground from its foundation by Thomas Lord in 1787 through to the twenty-first century stadium with its state-of-the-art media centre. Exciting matches and great events are brought to life in this remarkable book by former museum curator and MCC librarian Stephen Green.
0 7524 2167 0

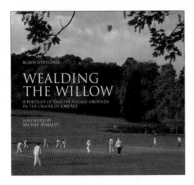

Wealding the Willow
ROBIN WHITCOMB

In many communities in South East England the local cricket ground is still at the very centre of village life. This book, featuring photographs, anecdotes and historical information, serves as a lasting record of some of these picturesque grounds across Kent, Surrey, Hampshire and East and West Sussex. Foreword by Richie Benaud.
0 7524 3457 8

If you are interested in purchasing other books published by Tempus, or in case you have difficulty finding any Tempus books in your local bookshop, you can also place orders directly through our website

www.tempus-publishing.com